More praise for
The How to Write a Book Book:

"Delightfully, this book is rich in flavor and word mastering as well as How To's. And then part 3 puts you in the pockets of established writers who tell their stories to inspire and challenge you to get busy adding your voice to this crazy-quilt world of writing. Bravo! Yvonne and Tom, as usual, your guidance and wisdom sharing is spot on!"

— Shawna Schuh, CSP, coach, speaker, and author of *51 Ways to Pick Up Your Get-Up-And-Go*

"I loved reading *The **How to Write a Book** Book* by Yvonne Divita and Tom Collins for a couple reasons. First, I loved the practical, relatable, easy-to-follow advice on writing, publishing, and marketing a first book in Parts 1 and 2. As a published author myself, I was then inspired by Part 3, Stories from the Trenches, with words of wisdom from experienced authors that got my energy revving on re-launching my first book, *Under the Rose-Colored Hat*, and starting my second one. Thanks to Yvonne and Tom, I'm more excited than ever before to make writing a constant part of my entrepreneurial life."

— Tracy Chamberlain Higginbotham, Founder, Women TIES, LLC, Speaker, and Author of *Under the Rose-Colored Hat*

"Wow, what a fabulous resource! Like millions of others, I've dreamt of becoming a published author. I enjoy writing, but that has always felt like a million miles from actually becoming an author! This wonderful book takes that fear away and breaks the process down into bite-sized chunks, with practical steps to take you from beginning to end. I recommend all aspiring authors read this and get started on their first book."

— Carol Hanson, CEO at CarolHanson.com, Image consultant and personal sylist

"The idea of writing a 'real' book can be daunting and overwhelming. Yvonne and Tom guide you through a step-by-step process from why and what to the all-important how. Filled with proactive advice, while cheering you on to success. "

— Toby Bloomberg, President of Bloomberg Marketing

"Aspiring authors ... quit planning to write your book. Get this one! Spend a weekend with it, get fired up, and get going!

"When Yvonne and Tom helped me with a book project some years ago, I put my trust in them and it paid off. And now you can get their expertise in the form of an easy-to-read book. They're the real deal.

"Succinct. Direct. Inspiring."

— Anita Campbell, Founder and CEO of Small Business Trends

"Yvonne DiVita and Tom Collins' *The **How to Write a Book** Book* is great primer for those writers who want a step-by-step process for bringing their authorial dreams to life. As someone who appreciates a good How-to, I was impressed by the thorough start to finish approach to publishing your first work.

"The authors' analogy of building a house is a great way to frame the need for conscious planning, solid foundations, and creative design in creating a successful publication. The stories and anecdotes from other authors highlighted the value of the advice offered by DiVita and Collins. I wish I had a detailed outline like this when I was writing my first book, and I will definitely be referring to this one when I embark on the construction of my second one."

— Katherine McGraw Patterson (KP), Business Strategy, Speaker, Founder of WEBO Network, author of *Lunching with Lions: Strategies for the Networking-Averse*

"Part 1 inspired me to write! I've never had a belief that I could write a book. However, this book provides guidance and a stepped process that shows you how to go from the burning of an idea to a full-blown book that will promote your brand, your business, by demonstrating your expertise.

"It's a game-changer for those of us who have a book in us, but don't know how to take the words from our hearts and minds to the page."

— Joanne Grobbelaar, Strategic Business Consultant and host of the *All In* podcast

"*The **How to Write a Book** Book* is a gem: Every story, every reference, and the guides it offers along the way make this book invaluable to the novice and affirming to the well-seasoned author. This book covers all the bases with wonderful, vital, essential insights and tips for producing your book."

— Lonnee Rey, host of the "Midlife My Ass, I'm just getting started!" podcast, and #1 International Best-Selling author of *Life lessons learned from a lousy mother*

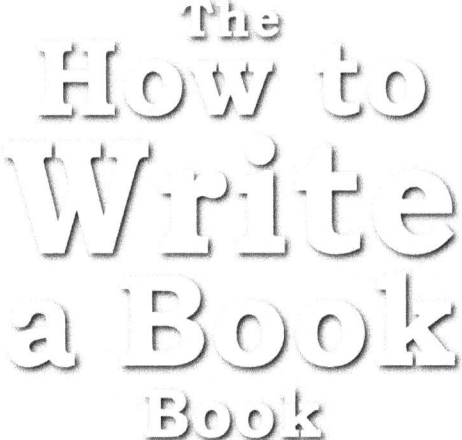

The How to Write a Book Book

Your Step-by-Step Plans for Bringing
BIG IDEAS to Life One Page at a Time

Yvonne DiVita & Tom Collins

WME Books
imprint of
Old Dog Digital, LLC
Binghamton, NY, USA

The ***How to Write a Book*** Book
Copyright © 2020 by Yvonne DiVita & Tom Collins

ISBN: 978-1-934229-38-5

Published in USA by
    Old Dog Digital, LLC, Binghamton, NY
    under its WME Books imprint

Editor: Yvonne DiVita
Interior & Cover Designer: Tom Collins

For special orders and bulk discounts contact:
    tom@OldDogLearning.com

Disclaimers:

While the authors and publisher have used their best efforts in preparing this book, they make no representations or warranties regarding the accuracy or completeness of the contents of this book or any related, referenced, or linked materials. The authors and publisher specifically disclaim any implied warranties of merchantability or fitness for a particular purpose, and make no guarantees whatsoever that you will achieve any particular result.

We believe all information, scientific research, and case studies and results persented herein are true and accurate, but we have not independently audited or confirmed the research methods, data collection, or results reported. Any advice or strategies contained in this book might not be suitable for your situation and you should consult your own advisors as appropriate.

Dedications

Yvonne's:

To my family. To my children who gave me incentive and encouragement and who continue to say, "You can do it, Mom!" To my brother and my three sisters, who act as if I am a rock star and tell everyone they know, "That's my sister!" And, especially, to my husband, Tom Collins, who tells me daily he is my biggest fan. Truth is, I am his biggest fan. He will always be my favorite pool boy.

Tom's:

To Yvonne, of course, always.

And – having previously thanked "all the authors of all the books" written so far (in *Read 'Em & Reap*) – I'll expand that here to all the authors of all the books **still to be** written, polished, and published!

Gratitudes

We remain grateful, of course, to the many folks we've thanked in our previous books, because their influences on us will always contribute to our work.

Focusing on direct contributions to this book, though, we want to celebrate our indebtedness to two groups:

For their amazing patience and their generosity in sharing their hard-won wisdom, the authors whose stories of lessons learned appear in Part 3: Guy Kawasaki, George Kittredge, Rosa Say, Robert W. Bly, Ellen Langas, David Young, Stephanie Siegrist, Michele Miller, Andrea Learned, Dick Richards, Amy Shojai, and Robbi Hess. Patience, because Yvonne has been collecting their stories for more than a decade and they've remained steadfast in their support for the project.

For their help in bringing the book to fruition and making it better by their insightful comments, our readers of the galley version: Toby Bloomberg, Anita Campbell, Joanne Grobbelaar, Carol Hanson, Tracy Chamberlain Higginbotham, Katherine McGraw Patterson, Lonnee Rey, and Shawna Schuh.

Contents

Introduction 1
  Books Bring Ideas to Life 3
  Pride and Accomplishment 4
  What to Expect from the How to
  Write a Book Book 7
    1. Information on the Writing Process 7
    2. Inspiration 7
    3. Advice on Book Marketing 8
    4. Advice on Publishing 8

Part 1

Book Building 13
  What could be easier than that? 13
  Five-step "Building" Process
    Step 1: The Idea! (your foundation) 15
    Step 2: Blueprints 16
    Step 3: Floorplans & "shop drawings" 17
    Step 4: Exterior Design 19
    Step 5: Interior Design, furnishings,
      as-built drawings & notes 22
  On Being Phenomenal 26
  Tips on Getting Help (hint: do you
    need a project manager?) 28

Part 2

Getting Started	33
Breaking Out of Writer's Block	39
The Power of a Visual World	45
To Justify or Not to Justify	53
And Now, a Word About Editing and Proofreading	67
Publishing Options: Mainstream or "Indie"	73
Marketing Tools and Tactics: Becoming "the Author of"	81

Part 3

Stories from the Trenches	97
We No Longer Live in the World of Dick and Jane, by Yvonne DiVita	101
Advice to Authors, by Guy Kawasaki	105
Sometimes a Book Just Happens, by George Kittredge	107
The Story Behind Managing with Aloha, by Rosa Say	113
A Fine Position to Be In, by Robert W. Bly	121
Keep On Writing, by Ellen Langas	127
How to Write a Book Under Extreme Duress, by David Young	129

How I Wrote Know Your Bones, by Stephanie Seigrist	133
It's Enough to Give You Gas, by Michele Miller	137
On Writing, by Andrea Learned	143
Lessons on Writing that I Keep Forgetting, by Dick Richards	147
7 Steps to Accidental Writer Success, by Amy Shojai	153
I dropped in a dragon, a car crash, a winning lottery ticket ..., by Robbi Hess	159
Best Laid Plans (Or, Writing Lessons from HGTV Stars), by Tom Collins	167
Index	175
About the Authors	185

Introduction

So, you want to write a book. Perhaps you've already started writing a book. Perhaps you have a finished manuscript and you're not quite sure what your next steps are - how to get it published and how to get it noticed so folks will buy it. Perhaps you're struggling with the question of how to publish it: eBook? Print book? Soft cover? Hard cover?

Let me go on the record saying I heartily approve of writing a book. It's my bold opinion that everyone has a book inside just waiting to get out. Anyone old enough to hold a crayon, a pencil, a pen, or a keyboard has dozens of compelling memories, experiences, and thoughts on life to contribute meaningful information to an audience of eager readers.

In fact, when I was in second grade, I was a prolific storyteller. I wrote stories and drew pictures to the exclusion of all else. This caused a good deal of dyspepsia in my mother – who was called in to the school on my account. She must have taken the teacher's lecture to heart and passed on the need to do second grade "work" as well as storytelling, because I somehow graduated from second grade and went on to complete my education accordingly. But I don't remember her visit, nor do I remember what she might have said to convince me to put my crayon down and pick up a pencil. Perhaps I put the crayon down, picked up the pencil, and just continued writing.

I do remember fifth grade – where I met Mrs. Mutz, my favorite teacher ever! It was she who encouraged me to continue writing and who made the biggest difference in my life. While returning an assignment to write a short story, Mrs. Mutz called me up to the front of the class to hand mine back, after she had given out everyone else's. I was petrified. What had I done wrong? Was it really so horrible? I could feel tears stinging the backs of my eyes.

She handed me my story and there it was: a great big red A+ at the top of the first page.

"This was a wonderful story," she smiled at me. "You're quite the writer, aren't you? This was the best story of all."

And then she hugged me.

That memory, those words of encouragement stayed with me and I visit them in memory almost every day. Someone in authority called me a writer! It gave me the courage to continue writing, to fight my demons and wrestle them to the ground every day (indecision, worry, the crumpled up pages of a dark story, thrown on the floor in anger).

And by staying true to that little girl who took her short story in her hands, held it to her chest, and treasured it as proof that she could, indeed, someday be a writer, I became what I am a today, a writer, a blogger, and a book coach.

I live to tell stories and to help others tell stories.

Books Bring Ideas to Life

Your book may be simmering deep in your heart, like a pot ready to boil. The subject may be something personal – such as a life-altering experience or an epiphany that changed your life for the better.

Your book idea may be a guide showing the steps you took to make a drastic career change, something that finally put you on the true path to happiness. It may be something you want to share with others, to help them take that leap of faith.

You may choose to write about your family history, putting it in a cultural perspective to give others an historical background of your national heritage.

You may even be writing the next great mystery story, or a teen angst novel.

Your book might be 50 pages or 1,000 pages – whatever it is – writing it sets you apart from the rest of the world.

Pride and Accomplishment

The satisfaction of putting your thoughts down on paper, of committing your words to print, whether with pen and paper or with fingers to keyboard, is the triumph of a lifetime. Every writer I've ever talked to – and I've talked to hundreds – talks about his or her book with pride and accomplishment, not merely for the creativity of the book idea, but for the satisfaction of completing the task.

Can you remember hiding a flashlight in your bed so you could read after dark – when your Mom and Dad thought you were sleeping? Or, lugging that 400-page library book with you on your family camping trip – because you only had 25 more pages left to read and you didn't want to wait 10 days to finish it?

Introduction

Maybe you were one of the kids who actually liked history, or math, and your fond memory involves stories about Alexander the Great, or the American Civil War, or trigonometry and how math is the answer to everything in the world (so math people tell me; I'm not convinced).

No matter what you remember – the smell of old books on library shelves, the feel of a new, just purchased tome from your local bookstore, or the excitement of the latest story in a series of bestselling novels – doesn't the memory put a smile on your face?

Isn't that the same kind of smile you want to see on the faces of people who read your book?

Here are some reasons people I know have written books. See if you relate to any of them:

- The book helped them define who they are by uncovering the reasons they did and do the things they do. The insight in their books, they said, was designed to help others like them make sense of the confusion in their lives, also.
- The book was a learning experience, helping the author understand the human condition, or the stock market, or how to tie a tie. Learning is inherent in writing and reading books—for writers as much as for our readers.

- The book was to jump-start a new career or to create a product for a speaking platform.
- The book was written to revive a career that seemed to be getting stale or boring.
- The book was written to introduce a new product or service or enhance an already existing one.

These books, as all books, are:

- inspirational and thought provoking
- educational and informative
- humorous and entertaining

A book can be about anything you want it to be. The value of the book is in its ability to touch others. The nice thing is, as the author, you get to choose who those others are – for the most part.

Becoming an author will transform you and your life. As soon as the world sees "Author of *Transforming Failure into Success*" next to your name (just an example, your book will be different), you become a new person. You become an instant celebrity with credibility, insight, expertise, and valued experience.

The transformation is immediate, but the success only comes with hard work. Are you ready?

What to expect from
The How to Write a Book Book

1. Information on the writing process – Yes, we said process. Forget the stereotypical, penniless writer sitting in a cold, bare attic, hidden from the world, scribbling his or her thoughts on ragged pieces of paper.

Today's writer is more likely to be putting fingers to keyboard, at a desk in a home office, on a dining room table, or at a local café that has wi-fi.

Regardless of where or how you write your book the truth is that writing is a process – just as much as building a house, crafting a boat, organizing a conference, building a website, or baking a cake. Leave out a step or an ingredient and – you risk ending up with a poor excuse for a house, a boat, a conference, a website, a cake, or a book.

2. Inspiration – You'll read the stories of other writers talking about how they came to write their books. They will share their experiences and inspire you to keep keeping on.

3. Advice on marketing – This book will share advice on ways to market your book, beyond the usual blather about writing press releases and sending out post cards. Can you say: 'blogging book tour' and 'podcasting?' How about swapping newsletters?

One of the most important lessons I learned when I wrote and self-published my first book was that my own efforts marketing my work were directly responsible for how many sales I made and the attention the work received. The publisher, a print-on-demand company, offered little help or advice, other than to court my pocketbook with incentives to 'buy' advertising in the NY Times. They did give me a 20+ page booklet about getting into bookstores and writing press releases, but, once the book was published, they really didn't care what happened to it.

It's much the same with traditional publishing, with a little twist. We'll discuss that in our section on marketing.

4. Advice on publishing – In today's print-on-demand world, self-publishing takes on a whole new meaning. We'll talk about the perceptions of self-publishing, about the realities of it, and throw out some questions you might want to ask yourself as you consider this growing method of publication. Yes, you need to format for Kindle.

I'll even add some information on approaching traditional publishers. I'll share my own thoughts and a bit of insight from across the desk, so to speak (real stories from authors who published with mainstream publishers).

Now, let's begin.

~ Yvonne DiVita

Note on the use of I/we in this book:
Yvonne started the project and had written a good deal of what you'll find in Parts 1 and 2 before Tom began working on it. We decided to leave many sections in her voice, because that felt right to both of us. We hope the switching back and forth is more of a help to understanding the source(s) of the advice, than any hinderance to the flow.

The **How to Write a Book** *Book*

Part 1

Book Building

> *"Begin at the beginning," the King said very gravely, "and go on until you come to the end, then stop."*
>
> ~ Lewis Carroll, *Alice in Wonderland*

What could be easier than that?

This quote, from *Alice in Wonderland*, isn't about writing a book. But it is about telling a story. Everything in life is a story. Did you know that?

Did you know that your conversations all day long, with friends, family, and strangers you meet here and there, are all part of a bigger story? A story that makes up who you are and why you exist. A story that brings people together, in a collective whole that speaks with one voice.

Why shouldn't it be your voice?

It's when you decide to put that story down on paper that the magic happens. And while eBooks are a large part of today's market, never doubt the true power of a print book. Many people will print that eBook, regardless of how many pages it is! Some of us still love that feel of paper in our hands.

Here's the truth, when you put your story down on paper, it becomes more than the short narrative you shared with someone over coffee. Or the 60-second commercial you recited at your latest networking event. It becomes a representation of you.

Putting your story in print announces who you are and what you are about more effectively than the outfit you wore that day (yes, people do judge you by how you dress). Your book brands you more effectively than a business card (I'm not saying don't have one, I'm saying, business cards get lost or discarded; books do not). It's even more effective than your website (your website is about the big picture, your book is the story of how that website came to be).

When it's done right, your book can increase income, bring you more and better clients, garner speaking engagements, open opportunities to more unique ways to make money, and set you up as an expert in your field of endeavor.

Book Building

Let's look at a five-step process we've created, to organize our writing for real success. This process shows how writing a book is very much like building a house.

Step one: The idea! (your foundation)

Your idea is your foundation. A foundation drives the kind of house/book by supporting the purpose of the task.

For a house, you could be building a ranch, a split-level, a Victorian, a center entrance Colonial, even a castle. For a book, you must ask yourself, is it going to be

- a novel
- a textbook
- an inspirational narrative with a moral of the story ending
- a business book
- or a book training folks to achieve a goal using your advice?

Just what kind of book is it? Understand that within each of these options, there are sub-options – for a novel, is it a romance or a mystery? For an inspirational narrative, is it for the general public or business folk? For training, is it a complete how-to on carpentry, or is it written about a useful tool we all use, that you know how to use better?

Step two: Blueprints

How many "rooms" are you planning for your house/book? Typically, a house has at least a kitchen, a living/family room, a dining room, two or more bedrooms, and two or more bathrooms. In a book, this is where you create your table of contents, with the first draft of your chapter titles.

If you know what kind of book you're writing, you'll be able to write chapter titles and short blurbs fleshing out what each will contain. From there, you can develop a more detailed outline, with subheadings and perhaps a sentence or two under each of those. If you're more visual, you could accomplish the same thing in the form of a story board, or a mindmap.

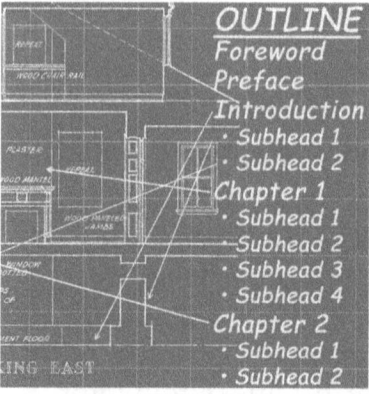

Either way, you'll be on your way with a framework that will be sort of a blueprint for you. Remember, it's just a first draft. You will be editing it as you go along.

Step three: Floorplans and "shop drawings"

How will the rooms of the house/book be arranged? In a house, you can choose a traditional layout, or you can work with your builder to get creative. In your book, some questions are: Will you begin with a flashback? Will the story flow in a chronological order? Will you have Part 1, Part II, Part III, in historical progression? Or, will you be eclectic and arrange your chapters in a design that might make your 4th grade teacher cringe, but will delight the readers of your book?

As you decide this, ask yourself, how will my book's *flow* work for the reader? Just as the occupants of the house are important to the builder, the readers of a book need to be important to a writer.

And you need to keep asking that question, again and again. As you frame out the rooms and hallways, start running plumbing, electric, and HVAC, does the floorplan really work? In construction, changes are almost always needed, requiring "shop drawings" to document (and pretest) the improvements.

Any sensible builder eagerly seeks ongoing input from the architect, or the owner, or the project manager, or the realtor who will be selling the house to get objective, honest feedback and answers to that crucial question: will this house, built with this revised plan, meet the homeowners' needs?

Likewise, as you add more flesh to the bare bones of your outline, keep asking *will this arrangement of content work for my readers?* And like the sensible book builder you are, seek objective, honest feedback from your editor, book coach, rough draft readers, and knowledgable friends and experts, asking them the same ultimate question.

Tap into these different individuals and groups at every stage, from the moment you decide to write the book to the moment it goes to the printer. Some will end up writing a foreword, review, or testimonial when you get near completion of the book.

Listen carefully to your inner voice and to those you're consulting. Be honest with yourself about the answers to *does this structure (still) work?* Be ready to adjust your book's floorplan, scribble revised outline entries, or rework the whole outline with your version of shop drawings, if those answers start looking like anything other than a resounding, yes!

Tom will have more to say about the need for a book to evolve throughout the writing process and the "shop drawing" analogy in his "Stories from the Trenches" entry at the end of this book.

But now, let's look outside.

Step four: Exterior Design

During the building of your house, you will be exploring how you want the outside to look. Depending on where you're building the choices could be all yours or largely dictated by an HOA (Homeowner's Association).

Think curb appeal. This includes both the architectural design of the house itself and the landscaping. These should make a visitor want to visit and provide welcoming access, via driveway and/or pathways.

With your book, you'll be thinking about your cover design:

- front cover, with attention-grabbing design, title, subtitle (nonfiction), and your name
- custom back cover, with a catchy headline, testimonials, a short bio, and your picture
- spine, with enough of the title to grab attention and your name

Why should you be considering, drafting, and rethinking these elements, in this order, throughout the book building process? We urge you to, as we have, watch people in a bookstore or library, particularly where there are displays of books with the front covers showing. You'll observe a nearly universal sequence of behavior that should drive how your cover is designed.

From ten or fifteen feet away, a person notices a particular book. Drawn by the overall design, which may include arresting graphics, the main title in huge typography, or instead feature the author's name, if by a sufficiently famous celebrity, they walk over to get a closer look.

The house analogy would be a person arriving for the first time on the street or sidewalk in front of your new home. Will the curb appeal draw them to your door?

When a reader does approach a book, if their interest is confirmed by the front cover elements that were not clear from a distance (e.g,, subtitle, awards, a testimonial), they pick up the book.

And . . . drumroll, please . . . they turn it over and scan the back cover. Different people will focus first on the headline, or the testimonials, or your bio or picture. But one or more of those elements needs to be compelling enough to reconfirm their interest.

Back to your house, the welcoming design of your front doorway, porch, seating, lighting,

Book Building

windows, all work together to confirm for the visitor their decision to knock or ring the bell.

Which leads to the third common step in this book-behavior sequence – they open the book. We'll get to what they'll do next in the next section, but a few quick reminders, first.

Don't forget the thumbnail! The majority of books are sold online. Your cover must not only grab attention from 15 feet away in a physical bookstore, it must do the same as a thumbnail on Amazon. Luckily, a good design that works in person should work similarly online. But make sure you view yours on a monitor, tablet, and phone screen to be sure.

Don't forget the spine! The spine is a separate design element. If your book is shelved among dozens of others with only the spines showing, that may be the only way of attracting a reader's attention.

Book cover design is incredibly important. If you're working with a designer, make sure they know what goes into book cover design. Not magazine covers. Not newsletter covers. Not Facebook covers.

BOOK covers.

Don't forget the marketing! Perhaps we should be hammering this on every page?

Remember what the King of Hearts said so gravely. *That* is where you will begin your marketing – at *the beginning*, not at the end. And continue marketing until you reach the end . . . oh, wait, you never will . . . so, you'll never stop.

Marketing happens in conjunction with all Five Steps, not separate from them.

Step five: Interior Design, Furnishings, As-Built Drawings and Notes

Will your house be so big that visitors will need a map to get around in it? Is it a castle? I know, it's your "castle," but is it really a large home with many rooms and hallways folks can get lost in? In public buildings, where lots of people need to get around as newcomers, we use signage, directories, color coding, perhaps a receptionist to help visitors find their way around.

In a house, once inside we tend to rely on familiar design and decorating elements as cues. When we enter, we likely expect to see into one or more rooms intended for gathering, like living room, family room, dining room, or kitchen. And the furnishings, appliances, and decor will instantly tell us which is which. Down hallways or upstairs, we may expect to find bedrooms, bathrooms, or other more personal spaces, intended for visitors less often.

If your house includes a home office or business area, you may well choose to add some signage, inside and out, to guide visitors. Our analogies to book building hold here, too.

In your book, the question of how long the book will be (word count or how many pages) is directly related to the story you are telling, or the information you are delivering. As a rule of thumb, the longer the book the more interior "signage" you'll want to provide, so your readers can easily and comfortably find their way around.

In this step, you will consider the need for such navigational tools as:

A detailed or expanded table of contents. This could mean including all your chapter subheadings, or providing a short summary of the content under each chapter. The second form could help even with a longer fiction book.

Informative chapter titles. Think of each chapter title as leading the reader forward through your book. This will help them, not only while they're reading, but from the first moment they see your TOC. Even in fiction, using only numbers for chapters may be a missed opportunity; one to be chosen consciously, at least.

Running page headers, with chapter titles. Standard running header design puts the book title on the left pages in the spread and the author's name on the right pages. In nonfiction books, however, we recommend putting chapter titles on the right pages. These are extremely useful to help readers refer back and forth as they learn from your work. Likewise, if they want to use it as a reference later.

An alphabetical topic index. An index can be done using software or hiring a professional. We recommend a professional. A software tool will not understand the nuances of your writing, no matter how good it is.

Endnotes. More and more, we see nonfiction books including useful reference sections, keyed to the pages in the text where the point is made. In fiction books, authors may choose to share some sort of historical note, biographical information about real or imagined characters, or pronunciation keys.

Other possibilities: bibliography, further reading lists, appendices, questionnaires, checklists, worksheets, and many more. We even see guides to help book clubs discuss the book.

Any or all of these tools may be helpful, even crucial, to your book being purchased, let alone read and appreciated. Think back to the bookstore, when the cover design got your book noticed, picked up, turned over, and finally opened.

Picking up on our book building analogy, this is the moment when you open the door and your visitor's first impression inside your home or office is made. Just as there are expectations about where the common areas are to be found, what kind of furnishings, appliances, or decor to look for, perhaps even whether some actual signage would be helpful, so it is with books.

Watching from nearby, it's impossible to know which patron looks at which element inside the book first. We suspect the TOC is most common, but have no hard evidence. Some may look at a foreword, preface, or introduction first. Some may look at the testimonials inside the front cover, or be guided by the TOC to a chapter, a chart, or an appendix that's of particular interest to the individual.

Their decision to purchase or borrow and read your book likely happens in these few moments. If you've built your book well, designed and decorated it with useful content and tools to meet their needs, if not delight their senses, you both win.

In the step 5 subheading, we mentioned "as-built drawings and notes" and we'll wrap up the five steps with this. During any building project, lots of changes from the original plans will occur. We talked about being open to these in your writing, too. And this editorial process of refinement, revision, and outright reorganization can remain in play right down the moment you upload your final print file to your publisher or platform.

A quality builder will deliver to the owner a set of as-built drawings and notes to show all the significant changes. These are invaluable to the owner when it comes time for repairs, remodeling, or additions.

As a quality book builder, you have an analogous task. As your book evolves into its final form, make sure your choices among the tools for navigation described in this section have evolved, too, and kept true to the needs of your readers.

On Being Phenomenal

We believe anyone can write a phenomenal book following these five steps. Sales of your book – your "success" if you will – depends heavily on how well you manage these Five Steps, and how you connect your readers to the finished product.

Success is also relevant to how you present the story in all the speaking engagements you'll get from publishing the book. Much of your success as a published author depends on how comfortable your audience feels with the overall design and production of your book, as well as how close the content is to meeting their needs and expectations.

Much like building a house, where people have expectations of the finished product and expect the contractor to deliver that product, writing a book says to your audience, "I get you. I know what you're facing. I have the solutions. You can depend on me."

You want readers to be as awe-struck by your book as homeowners are by their new house. Remember: readers pick up a book in a bookstore or see it online and have immediate expectations of what the book should do for them. At the very least, for most non-fiction, it needs to solve a problem that has been nagging them for a long time.

If you're writing fiction, your book needs to entertain, take me away from the busy, overwhelming world of "now" and also be internally believable, regardless of genre. We call this, "suspension of disbelief." If I cannot get lost in the story, I will likely move on to something else.

Just recently I was reading a novel that was humorous and somewhat entertaining, but it didn't live up to its promise of mystery and intrigue, and I never finished it.

Also, don't get crazy trying to imitate Agatha Christie, Nora Lofts, Dashiell Hammett, Michael Hyatt, Kathleen Gage, Katherine McGraw Patterson, or Debbie Allen – or any other author – because you love their style.

Be yourself.

Follow the advice of 19th century German philosopher, Arthur Schopenhauer, writing on style:

> **"Truth that is naked is the most beautiful, and the simpler its expression the deeper is the impression it makes."**

Oh, and if you don't recognize some of the names listed above, they're all writers we both appreciate. You can easily find out more about them on Amazon.

Tips on Getting Help (hint: do you need a project manager?)

Study writing, on your own, or with a group. In my hometown of Rochester, NY, there is a small company called Writers and Books, which exists to help writers become better at their craft. Established authors teach new, aspiring writers the ins and outs of becoming a published author.

If you don't have a similar organization in your hometown, why not start one?

Book Building

And, of course, take or audit writing courses at your local adult-ed, University, or Community College.

At the very least, you can start a book club on Facebook.

Or come join my "Smart Women Write Books" group on Facebook. Tom's "Read More" group, too. We'd be delighted to have you.

As one more nod to the house building analogy, for many homeowners, their best friend during construction is their project manager – a pro who can make sure the work is progressing smoothly and being done right. If a problem arises, or changes to the plans need to be made, the project manager provides advice to the homeowner, helping to guide their choices along the way.

Consistent with our analogy, for a quality builder a project manager should be a valued ally in designing, redesigning, and delivering the finished product that meets all of the owner's needs. For a quality book builder, the role of project manager matches that of an experienced book pro: the book coach.

Whether you need a book coach depends on factors similar to construction work: the size and complexity of the project and the level of industry experience of the builder (and the audience/owner). For a substantial book, if you're not experienced in all the design, editorial, and publishing platform roles we've discussed, consider whether a book coach would help you bring your book writing project to fruition more effectively. And more in keeping with the brand you're building as author or authority.

In **Part 2**, we'll dig deeper into the work of getting your book written, published, and into the hands of your readers.

Let's go back and begin, of course, at the beginning with: Getting Started

~ Yvonne and Tom

Part 2

Getting Started

"It had long since come to my attention that people of accomplishment rarely sat back and let things happen to them. They went out and happened to things."

~ Elinor Smith

While it's often helpful to have a mentor or book coach before you write that first word – it's not mandatory. Since you've got this book and have come this far, Yvonne will play your book coach here, to give you a feel for how that works for you.

Commit to Writing, Digitally, Daily

As any writing teacher or coach will tell you, successful writers write EVERY DAY.

So, get settled at your computer – you are planning to write this on a computer, aren't you? It's all well and good to cling to the old Dick and Jane world of the 20th century, using a pen and paper, or manual typewriter. I love pen and paper, too. But eventually you will have to convert your text to digital format, or the printer will not be able to print it.

Prepping for Print

Speaking of the printer, if you're planning on "indie" publishing, through a local printing company, Amazon's KDP, Ingram Spark, or any of the other online book publishing platforms, you're going to have to learn enough to create and upload a press-ready PDF file.

Almost all book printing these days will require some variation of PDF file. Your chosen printer will provide specs for things like bleeds, printer's marks, and so on.

In most cases, you'll also need to produce a separate, high resolution digital file for your cover. The combined image must arrange the back cover, spine, and front cover correctly for the size and thickness of your book.

Join the 21st century. Buy a computer or hire a typist, then plan on sending your chapters and/or the completed manuscript via e-mail to your editor, proofreader, or publisher. They may request a hard copy also, but a digital copy of your manuscript is vital to being taken seriously today.

Easier Editing

Having a digital copy also saves time – at every stage of the writing and publishing process – email attachments or uploading to document sharing sites like Google or Dropbox are much faster than snail mail.

Your book coach will require digital copies, also, throughout the writing and editing process. That's so she can enter her comments, suggestions, and markups to the file, where you'll be able to see them in context. Then you can discuss her input with the document on both your screens. And you can easily adopt, copy/paste, rewrite, edit – or even delete – her advice!

Go on, get settled at your computer and start typing. Don't fret about grammar and punctuation for now. Whatever word processing program you use will likely have a spelling and a grammar checking function. While it's suicide to rely solely on these computer programs to keep your work honest, allow them to guide you as you write your first draft.

Yes, you can shout and swear at your word processing program. It won't mind. I think most of them expect it.

The Beginning: Text or TOC?

If you're not totally immersed in the story – fictional or otherwise – just begin at the beginning: with the table of contents and go forward from there. A table of contents is much like an outline, something you learned to do in grade school.

I expect you can come up with a basic table of contents, even if you were never any good at making outlines. If you're stumped, revisit Step 2 in our Book Building model and, if you're more visual, consider starting with a story board or mindmap. You may also want to download our free *Book as Business Card* eBook for advice on moving forward.

Throughline: "Electrifying" Your Idea

As you begin, we recommend adapting the concept of a throughline from Chris Anderson's book, *TED Talks: the Official TED Guide to Public Speaking.* In simple terms, the throughline is the theme that ties together every element in your book.

You might think of the throughline in our house building analogy as the wiring systems that connect and energize every part of the structure. All the appliances, lights, tools, communication devices – heck, even many pieces of furniture these days – need to plug into the wiring to work.

Getting Started

As Anderson explained in a 2016 Fast Company interview, you should be able to state your throughline "in no more than 15 words." Don't be lulled by such simplicity. Those words need to carry "robust content" and provide some "unexpectedness." He gave a few examples, like:

- More choice actually makes us less happy.
- Vulnerability is something to be treasured, not avoided.

With devices in your home, anything you plug in must be compatible with or supported by the system. For your book, every topic, example, or story must connect with and support your throughline.

Writing, Not Engraving

Don't be surprised if your table of contents changes as you get into the book. It's merely a guide and sometimes you need to pivot on your journey to the end. Be ready to do so.

A few talented writers may stick with their original TOC, but most folks I've worked with did edit or reorganize their TOC during the writing process. An ability to be flexible will guarantee less worry as you go forward with your writing.

In fact, technology has made it so much easier to make last minute changes to manuscripts, you should never worry about getting it right the very first time. Recognize that you'll likely make many changes, as you move through your work.

Those of us who harken back to those old 20th century days, remember how unkind typewriters were in allowing us to easily and quickly revise our manuscripts. Today, we love having the ability to make changes and/or corrections as easily as it is to write the wrong thing to begin with!

That Word Again, Commit!

If you are immersed in the story – fictional or otherwise – begin where you will, and write, write, write. Yes, write every day!

Every day – at least a page. Set yourself up for success with a word count commitment:

> **"I will write 500 or maybe 5000 words every day!"**

I counsel you, do not vary from this task. Write every day – even if it's nothing more than notes to yourself about the story.

Build the habit of writing. Keep the spark of inspiration alive. Make this journey one of excitement, full of trials and tribulations, but also full of passion, joy, and accomplishment.

~ Yvonne and Tom

Breaking Out of Writer's Block

"Actions speak louder than words but not nearly as often."

~Mark Twain

I've experienced writer's block a few times, usually when life invades my writing time and sends me off in a different direction. In fact, this little book gave me several moments of writer's block – from beginning to end.

While I agree with Mark Twain, I also know that overcoming writer's block is a trial of sorts, in which we are each tested and stomped on, sometimes.

Yes, writer's block can feel impossible to break – and ever more so at those times you aren't even sure what you're experiencing is writer's block! As opposed to just having a poor story idea. Or being distracted by normal things like a crying baby, a sick relative, or a cat with hair-balls.

Is it writer's block? Or just life getting in the way?

Even Stephen?

I have often wondered if prolific writers suffer from writer's block, or if writer's block is no worry to them, because they never run out of material? Do writers such as Joyce Carol Oates, Stephen King, Malcolm Gladwell, Michael Hyatt, Mark Twain, Norah Lofts, just to name a few, suffer the sting of writer's block as they compose their best-selling books? Would they even tell us, if they did?

Wait, I believe Stephen King *did* tell us in his excellent book on writing, descriptively called *On Writing*. Great book. Get it. Read it. His writer's block solution is to add a new problem. Interesting, yes?

We writers who are mere mortals deal with this issue over and over again. In all of the writer's workshops I've attended or taught, writer's block rears its ugly head at some point.

If you're like me, or like the person next to you in your writer's group, or so much like any writer sitting at their computer on a sunny Wednesday morning, the day after completing an especially difficult chapter in your book, staring at the monitor as if you expect it to talk to you, give you gentle advice, or permission to go back to bed, you understand the terror of writer's block.

The best advice I can give you is to accept that it happens to us all, and to follow Mark Twain's advice and GET MOVING.

I also wrote a post about this on my Nurturing BIG IDEAS blog. Here's the gist of that post:

Breaking out of DREADED writer's block

1. Some writers get inspiration from reading (even re-reading) a favorite author. Others think you should avoid reading at all – in fear of having what you're reading influence your own work. Still others think that reading something totally different than what you're writing, is the answer.

Personally, I think the more you read, the better you write, no matter what.

My personal preference is to read fiction. Fiction inspires me to write, no matter what kind of writing I'm doing at the moment. Fiction stimulates my brain and nudges me to get at the computer and start typing. "Yes," it whispers to me, "you, too, can be a published author."

Generally, that's because I believe I can write as well as any of the fiction authors I read. Blasphemy in some way? Perhaps. But, also, truth.

2. Scour the local newspaper, or the last seven issues of USA Today or reread a favorite online newsletter. Read the NY Times or the Washington Post. Shift your focus from your own work, to the news of the day.

Try to find news stories that might support what you're writing.

Your aha! moment will appear – if you're patient. Yes, you can check Facebook ... for inspiration, nothing else. Facebook will eat you alive, if you let it. It's more "buy this buy this" than anything else these days.

3. Put the current work in a drawer and start something new. Write fresh content for a fresh story. By taking your focus off the worrisome work, your subconscious will begin to do its magic, and you will discover the answers you seek.

Plus, you'll have a new story to work on when you finish your current project. At the very least, you will have an opening to a blog post.

4. Rework your table-of-contents or your outline. This gives you a chance to reconnect with the material.

5. Take a break. A few minutes or an afternoon. Get a latte, jog around the park,

visit a friend, bake blueberry muffins, ask a relative how the kids are.

Bring some life back into your life.

It might spark renewed interest in what you're writing, or at least reveal why you're having trouble connecting with the words.

* * * * * *

Tom has one more "relevant distraction": Give some thought to those navigation aids that we talked about in Part 1. Will readers need an index to better access your ideas? A paged reference list? For fiction, a historical note? Maps of the fantasy realm?

Thinking about how your reader might need help to engage fully with your work may well jolt you into action again, to get writing!

* * * * * *

Last advice on this topic, from novelist and poet, Barbara Kingsolver:

> **"I learned to produce whether I wanted to or not. It would be easy to say oh, I have writer's block, oh, I have to wait for my muse. I don't. Chain that muse to your desk and get the job done."**

~ Yvonne and Tom

*The **How to Write a Book** Book*

The Power of a Visual World

"The wrappers in which things come not only powerfully affect what interests us but also how we react to the contents we find inside."

~Alex Lickerman, M.D.
in Psychology Today, Aug 2012

Yes, Virginia, people do judge a book by its cover.

What? You know better than to judge a book by its cover? You've read plenty of good books that had atrocious covers? Good for you. The rest of your reading audience is not so perceptive.

Studies show that people like good design and especially good cover design. Your readers see the cover first, after all.

There is no denying we live in a visual society. Since the advent of the world wide web, our world has become even more visual.

Alex Lickerman, in his article in Psychology Today, August 26, 2012, said,

> *"... if anyone doubts how their expectations for a book they're about to read are affected by its presentation, I'd challenge them to examine their initial reaction to a book not with an unattractive cover but with an amateurish one."*

In most cases, because the cover of your book is the first thing people see, it needs to stir them emotionally or intellectually. When asked how a cover influences the reader, the answers I've received have varied:

"I have to feel it."

"I have to like it."

"I don't know."

The "I don't knows" are drawn to the design, whether they understand it or not. They just can't describe why.

In some instances, a person or a person's face is what attracts the reader. Or, it's a color that draws their eye. Or, it's how the title sits on the page.

I don't care if your book is about quantum mechanics, or worm-farming, it needs to connect emotionally with the potential reader to spark interest. The first way it does this is by having a creative, relevant cover design.

The Power of a Visual World

I'm not going to belabor the point here – I'll just cite a few examples and let you decide whether or not the cover had any impact on the book's success:

No Logo by Naomi Klein: Notice how the cover demonstrates the title: no logo. It's plain, stark, and forceful. The letters in the author's name that spell the word 'no' are in red, as is the word 'no' in the title.

The rest of the cover is black, except for "Logo" and the other letters in the author's name, which are white. All for effect.

This book is true to its purpose from the beginning: No Logo ... nothing else needs to be said for interested parties to pick it up and flip through it.

Stephen King's book cover from *On Writing*, almost dismisses the idea of a colorful, intriguing, attractive book cover. But, let's pause that thought and really look at the design.

First of all, Stephen King is among the most recognizable writers on the planet, in my bold opinion (why be humble?). Anyone who loves his work and sees a cover with his image in it, and his name, is drawn to the book, like bees to honey.

47

But I want to go beyond how the image of him sitting at what I assume is his desk, draws us in. Let's look at the entire picture: the room, cluttered, much like mine (and yours?); the dog – seriously, everyone loves dogs; the fact that he's got his feet up and he's clearly editing a manuscript.

If the *On Writing* cover is not intriguing to you, I have to assume you're not a Stephen King fan. And that's okay. I merely want you to understand, the lack of color was purposeful, the pose was purposeful, and leaving the dog in was purposeful. You know why.

A Chick in the Cockpit: my life up in the air, by Erika Armstrong is an example of pretty good cover. It tells you that the story involves an airplane. The title tells you the story is about Erika's life in the cockpit, and the white background with a plane taking off simulates flight.

All is good there. However, this book is a true story turned into a bit of a novel. It's funny, sad, inspirational, and full of insight into the world of today's pilots – those captains who fly us all over the world, and into Erika's escape from domestic violence.

The Power of a Visual World

For me, what's missing is Erika's presence on the cover. It's her story from start to end. The memoir aspect of the story is a powerful part of it and that too is missing from this cover. I enjoyed the book but continue to feel the cover does not do it justice.

How did I come to read the book? It was given to us at a networking event. Erika was the speaker. I read the book because she was so impressive. I do not think I would have picked the book up at the bookstore, and certainly not online, just by the cover. I would have immediately been intrigued if her face was on the cover.

A more recent book for me, fiction, is Paula Munier's book, *A Borrowing of Bones*. Without even seeing the cover you know this is a mystery. If you're not intrigued by the title, I submit you're not well and should see a doctor.

On to the cover. We see a woman with a large dog. Looking off into the sunset. Or sunrise. I am not sure. They are either on a very high hill or on a mountain. It's all very mysterious, as it's meant to be.

I am at once drawn in and want to know whose bones they are borrowing. Don't you?

That is what you want your readers to feel.

Since the best is always saved for last, Sheryl Sandberg's book, *Lean In*, is an excellent example of a fantastic book cover that stands the test of time.

Let's face it, faces sell product.

Most of us know who Sheryl Sandberg is, much as we know who Stephen King is. Putting her picture on the cover, smiling invitingly, does two things: it attracts the right audience and it builds her brand.

The white background serves to highlight the book's title, it's sub-title, and her name. The red bar at the bottom that notes its best seller status draws the eye in to share that accomplishment, but it isn't overpowering.

This immediately draws me in. I will lean in, thank you.

I've seen covers where the author or publisher overpowered the space with its best seller status. That immediately turns me off.

When the title of your book works with the book cover design, you are already on your way to published success. Let me advise you to consider using your face on the cover of your book, regardless of your fame.

Your story is what you're writing, let the world see who the story is about. Being proud of sharing both your face and your story, creates an immediate emotional bond to your audience.

*　*　*　*　*　*

Both as a wrap to the topic of cover design and transition to our next topic, interior book design, we invite you to take time to watch Yvonne's recent *Smart Woman Conversations* interview with book designer Deanna Estes: https://www.nurturingbigideas.com/2020/04/books-design-front-cover-spine-and-back-cover-with-deanna-estes.html

They talked about everything from front to spine to back covers, fiction and nonfiction cover differences, colors, fonts, and the marketing functions of covers.

Oh, and interior book design rules, as well. That's where we turn next.

~ Yvonne and Tom

To Justify, or Not to Justify

That is the question.

Here's the short answer, a quote from a blog post Tom first published fifteen years ago:

> **"There isn't much justification for justified text."**
>
> ~ Prof. Ruth Ann Robbins, article: *Painting with Print*

We'll come back to justified margins. But let's first take a look at page layout, or, the overall visual impact of the inside of your book.

This page, for example, employs many visual elements: the font(s) used; sizes of the fonts; use of bold, italics, and bold-italics; the spacing of characters, lines, and paragraphs; first-line indents; left, centered, and right text alignments; the page margins, header, and footer as white space. Oh, and left-aligned, or "ragged-right" text.

Omitted from this page, by choice: the header text and footer decoration and page numbering found on most pages throughout this book. These design omissions by Tom serve to mark the beginning of each chapter.

You might also choose familiar elements like large, sometimes ornate drop caps in the first paragraph, first line SMALL CAPS, chapter numbering, and even the word Chapter itself. We want to help readers orient themselves instantly, through these visual cues, that they're about to enter a new topic.

Graphic elements

When thinking page layout, you must also include the possibility of images, charts, tables, and in some cases, cartoons. These items must be "placed" properly on the page. The main goal is to display any graphic element – photograph, drawing, table, chart, callout text, or any element not part of the main text – where it provides the most value to your reader.

We've all seen books and articles full of references like "see Table 3f, on page 267" when we're on page 260. Maybe we've been guilty of using such a reference scheme in our own writing. And we should feel guilty, if so, because this method violates the "adjacent in space" rule.

Haven't heard of that rule? Here's the explanation in an excerpt from Tom's 2003 NYS bar journal article, *Beyond Words: The Role of Graphics in Legal Writing*:

. . . Few design flaws are more irritating and distracting to the reader – and thus destructive to communication – than placing the graphic on a different page from the text that refers to it. [Edward] Tufte calls this keeping words and pictures "adjacent in space, not stacked in time." His references to space and time are significant.

Violating this rule wastes the reader's precious time. By disrupting the reader's concentration, it risks loss of attention. Separating words and pictures wastes space, too, forcing the use of references like "see Fig. 5-7" and the addition of boxes and captions to remind the reader that this graphic relates to a point made somewhere else, not in the text on the page where it happens to be found.

"Adjacent in space" is as close to a rigid rule as you will find in information design.

Image quality

We often treat two distinct qualities of text design, legibility and readability, as if they were synonymous. But as explained in the book design text, *Bookmaking*, legibility makes text *possible* to read, while readability makes it *comfortable* to read.

Similarly, when using graphics we can think of placement on the page as relating to making the image *comfortable* to digest its relationship to the text. Image quality relates to making it *possible* to understand the meaning and purpose of the image.

Placement and quality of images intersect, of course, just as various aspects of font selection and size affect both legibility and readability. Here we'll address just a few aspects of image quality.

Resolution. For digital images and printers, the density of the dots that make up the image is expressed as dots per inch, or dpi. The more dots per inch, the better your image will look.

Simple rules:

- For printed books, make sure your image software can produce at least 300 dpi images (more, if possible).
- For ebooks or web content, you can go as low as 72 dpi (though ebook readers, tablets, and phones are now capable of much better quality, so here again, more is better).

The resolution of graphics is critical to how they will ultimately look once the page is set and the printer (or the reader) prints it. Even with an ebook, Yvonne will often print it out, using grayscale to save on printer ink. If the image is sharp, grayscale will not matter. If the image is not sharp it will not print well and can impact the overall impression of the page, the book, and the author.

Dimensions. This refers to both the size of the image and its orientation. To make the information (e.g., numbers in a table, lines on a graph, or faces in a group photo) both "legible" and "readable" an image will have limits on how small it can be displayed.

The outer boundary will be the size of the page, although in extreme cases a foldout might be called for. In most cases, though, you'll want to be able to size the image to allow for the main text to share the page (adjacent in space, remember). This means taking into account placement possibilities, like wrapping the text around the image, or placing the image centered with text above and below.

Color. Unless you are publishing as an ebook only, you'll want to be able to convert your images to grayscale. For printing, you'll also want to control the brightness of your images, because generally the printer image will come out somewhat darker than it looks on your monitor.

Look for image editing software with the ability to adjust color values like brightness, contrast, hue, saturation, levels, and curves. We won't get into the specifics of these adjustments, because different software handles them differently, if at all. Find out which your software has and play!

Brief aside: This brings up the *necessity* for print proofs of your book. The caution about how a grayscale inside image may change when printed on a commercial press goes in spades for your cover. Plus, it may be your only chance to adjust your spine-width.

If a printer or online platform can't or won't provide you with print proofs of your book, before you sign off and set it live for sale, run the other way. Digital galleys or proofs that can only be reviewed on screen, or by desktop printing, will not let you really see your book as it will look and feel in your readers' hands.

Briefer aside: Some printers may still badger you about the "color space" or "color mode" of your image files, meaning RGB vs. CMYK. Unless they are using really old presses, or you are really anal about such things, keep your images in whichever mode you found them. Here's the advice from the Adobe InDesign Secrets folks:

> Fast forward to Modern times: Current print workflows perform excellent conversions of RGB to CMYK, and some printing processes – such as digital presses and large-format inkjet output – actually provide *better and more vibrant output* when fed with RGB content.

Image format. Your image software will likely allow you to save or export images in a number of file formats. This is another topic where you'll need to check with your printer or online platform about their requirements.

Digital images fall into two classifications: vector or raster. Vector images are composed of mathematically defined paths, so they can be scaled to very large sizes without losing any image quality. Vector images will have .eps, .ai, .svg, or sometimes .pdf filenames.

Raster images are made up of "dots" – actually, tiny squares – so they have very limited ability to be scaled larger than the original. Raster filename extensions include .jpg or .jpeg, .gif, .png, .tiff, and .bmp.

Since almost all photographs you'll work with will be raster images, this is where you'll need to pay attention to the dpi, or resolution, as well as the dimensions, of the original image. If you start out with a 72 dpi photo that is 1 inch wide by 1.5 inches tall (say, a book cover thumbnail), you will not have much luck enlarging it to display as a half-page demo image in a book about cover design. The result will be too grainy, or pixelated, and look even worse when printed.

Some software can "resample" a raster image and simulate (guess-timate?) the location and color of the new dots being added to generate a higher resolution image. Tom uses the technique in Adobe Fireworks; but even then, you'll want to start with as large an original as you can find.

Rough rule of thumb: To take a 72 dpi image up to a 300 dpi print-ready version, you'd want the original to be *about four times larger*. Thus, if you wanted the 300 dpi image to display on the printed page as a 2x3 inch photo, you'd need to start with an 8x12 inch, 72 dpi original.

But remember, resampling is still just the software's best approximation of a higher resolution. Bottom line: start with the highest quality images you can.

Unjustifiable

Justified text, or "fully" justified, means text that lines up perfectly on both sides.

Don't do it.

Why not? In one word: readability.

True, decades of research studies have been called inconsistent or inconclusive, when it comes to speed and comprehension of reading justified vs. ragged right text. The inconsistencies, however, seem to show either no difference, or better speed and comprehension with ragged right.

But there seems to be wide agreement that the real culprits in justified text have nothing to do with the straightness of the right margin. The readability problems for justified text come

To Justify, or Not

from what the typesetting software does to achieve it: "rivers" and excessive hyphenation.

Rivers in text refer to the overly wide spaces between words as the software adjusts to make the lines even. These spaces often line up vertically through two or more lines of text, causing distraction as the eye moves across the page. Similarly, the software can adjust the character spacing within words, requiring another bit of effort as readers scan for the patterns that form words into ideas. Lastly, the software by default will hyphenate words, which . . . well, let's look at some stark examples from the leading text, *Bookmaking: Editing | Design | Production*:

This image excerpt from a discussion of letterspacing shows the unhappy options when a page layout designer insists on justified text. You're stuck with bizarre gaps in the first one; bizarre letterspacing in the second one (third line); or hyphens at the end of 3 out ot 6 of the lines in the last one (50%).

Ironically, this bible of the publishing industry itself stuck with justified text, showing 7 hyphens among the 17 lines of main text showing to the left of the "bad" examples. That's 41%, only a small gain.

61

Tellingly, the solution they propose is to

> ... use the computer's refined tracking (letterspacing) and justification functions to make minute letter and word space adjustments throughout the text ...

Really? On this topic, we prefer the more realistic advice from another leading resource, *Dynamics in Document Design*. After noting how many settings are needed to control letterspacing, word spacing, hyphenation, and justification,

> ... often the designer must go back into the file and manually space some of the lines. ... What a pain!

The author further notes that in addition to improved readability, there is evidence that readers may simply prefer ragged right, at least in some nonfiction, technical settings (citing a NASA survey where 61.5% preferred ragged right over justified margins).

In the end, for the simple reason that both letters and words vary in width, justified text cannot be achieved without either uneven spacing or excessive hyphenation, or both. Hence, our subheading, *unjustifiable*.

For your readers' sake and your own sanity, just don't do it.

"But . . . but . . . what if some traditionalist thinks my book looks . . . unpolished . . . unprofessional . . . ragged?" you might ask.

Ragged beauty

We'll leave you with this quote and images from Tom's 2005 blog post, *No Justification*:

> Take a look at some of the most beautiful, well-designed books produced in the last couple of decades:
>
> Edward Tufte's series of books on information design (especially *The Visual Display of Quantitative Information*, 2nd ed., pg. 21, and *Visual Explanations*, pg. 79):

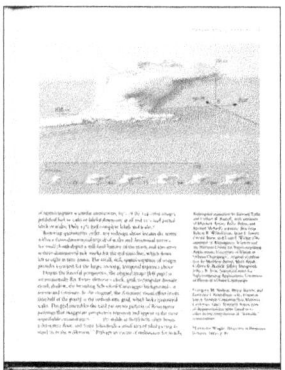

> and Douglas Holleley's wonderful resource for self-publishing, *Digital Book Design and Publishing*, pg. 45:

*The **How to Write a Book** Book*

Since it's my soapbox, here are a couple more examples (note: these authors are **information designers** writing about how to get your message across):

Dynamics in Document Design, by Karen Schriver (Wiley 1997), pg. 269:

Information Design Desk Reference, by Christine Sevilla (Crisp 2002) [to drive home her point, she shows you the even worse sin of right-only justification], pg. 59:

A more recent criticism aimed at academic publications insisting on justified margins put it this way:

> any advantages that one may perceive to be achieved by using fully justified full-page lines, fall to the wayside when it is realized that by doing so you are challenging the basic neurophysiology of comprehension.

The author of this critique is an editor and "a neuroscientist by academic training." He goes on, referring to the combined effect of justified text with the distractions caused by unpredictable line, character, and letter spacing, explaining

> the time it takes for the eye to [shift] from anchors on the right side of the page to the left side, find the next line anchor, interpret the pattern, and continue reading, while adjusting for any related confusion, affects the quality of neuronal input, short-term memory processing and consolidation, and language comprehension.

Donald Samulack, guest post on the Scholarly Kitchen blog: *Reflections on Text and Language Perception, and the Ramifications for Publishing Workflows* (Aug. 17, 2018).

It's your book. Don't let a publisher, printer, or pundit talk you into a design that interferes with your readers' experience.

~ Yvonne and Tom

Editing and Proofreading

Let's get real for a moment about editing and proofreading. It's been said that the lawyer who defends himself has a fool for a client. Such can be said for the writer who proofs and edits his or her own work.

Don't do it!

Your eyes are already trained to overlook misspellings, poor grammar, and errors in punctuation. If you have places in your book where you break the rules for effect, that's fine. Tell your editor and proofreader. They will understand.

They will also let you know whether they think the reader will understand.

What they do

Let's also look closer at the roles your editor(s) and proofreader should play. Yes, you may need more than one kind of editor. Yvonne covers some of the definitions in her free ebook, *Your Book as Business Card*, so here are the basics:

Copy editing:

"The tasks involved in copy editing include checking written material for grammar, spelling, style, and punctuation issues before it's prepared for proofreading. A copy editor may also do a rewrite, if necessary, to fix any problems with transitions, wordiness, jargon, and to ensure the style of the piece fits with the publication. This work is known as revision."

~ from Grammarly.com

Developmental editing:

"[A]n examination of all the elements of your writing, from single words and the phrasing of individual sentences, to overall structure and style. It can address plot holes or gaps, problematic characterization and all other existing material.

. . . .

"Good developmental editing will also bear in mind your target audience and will judge your work in relation to professional industry standards and expectations. Only once your manuscript has been cut, reshaped, revised, and developed will it be ready for a copy edit and proofread."

~ from Reedsy.com

Proofreading:

When the material gets close to a finished product, meaning it has been edited, laid

Editing and Proofreading

out, and designed, the proofreader searches for typographical errors. The proofreader works with a facsimile of a finished product, or a proof (hence the term proofreading). Proofreaders don't suggest major changes to the text; rather, they look for minor text and formatting errors and confirm the material is ready for publication.

~ from Grammarly.com

We recommend getting independent, objective, professional help with all these functions. There are times when an editor can fill both roles, as developmental editor and copy editor.

Yvonne offers an example of how a developmental editor works:

I once had a book client who kept repeating a phrase over and over and over until I finally said, "STOP! We are not using that phrase again. Not now, not ever again."

"I like that phrase," he whined.

"Your reader is sick of it," I said.

The phrase was sent to publishing hell.

That's how collaborating with an editor should work. Why have one, unless you're going to accept their judgment, especially when they stand in for your readers.

Maybe even stand *up* for your readers!

The proofreader role comes very near the end of the process. It should be assigned to an experienced professional, who brings fresh eyes to your work. Nowhere does the "fool for a client" rule apply more than proofreading.

To these professional roles, remember to add the cover design and page layout tasks we've discussed. And there's the commercial printer or online platform that will produce your physical books. Now let's add one more: a **book coach**.

Put me in, Coach!

We offer our own definition of the book coach role. It's the one described in Part 1, as analgous to the project manager on a house building project. Hired by you, the author, your book coach brings a range of writing and publishing experience. This enables them to serve as your guide and liaison among all the other roles and services needed to complete your book building project.

In some cases, a project manager may put on their tool belt and pitch in to fill one or more of the roles needed. That's how we see the book coach role, too. Your collaborative partner, helping out where needed to get the job done.

Mistakes still happen

We will admit to you that even with professional help, books get printed with mistakes. We human beings are not mistake-proof. But what then?

Enter the question: traditional publisher or indie publishing?

With a mainstream publication, you're stuck with that mistake forever. Few books make it to second printing, so the initial run of however many thousands will carry any mistakes to every bookstore shelf and to every reader the book is sold to.

It's not the writer's fault, of course. But those mistakes taint the reader's impression of you, nonetheless. Not that long ago, Yvonne worked with a writer whose NAME was misspelled on the cover of her book. To which her publisher said, "Well, we got it right on the copyright page."

Had she self-published with a print-on-demand model, only the initial run of books would have the mistake in them, a run which is oftentimes less than 100 copies. Once an error is discovered in a self-published, POD book, it can be fixed before any new copies of the book are printed.

The indie publishing model does set a higher standard for authors. You'll take full responsibility to make sure your end product is professionally produced.

But then, who better? You *will* be held accountable for your book's quality, whether you handed it over to a traditional publisher, did it all yourself, or assembled a team to get the job done right.

~ Yvonne and Tom

Publishing Options: Traditional or Indie Press

> *"If [a mainstream publisher] likes your book, they'll pay you a teeny tiny bit of money so you can rewrite the book to fit their mold and compromise your integrity, because publishers only care what sells, not what's good."*
>
> ~ Scott Ginsberg, That Nametag Guy

Today, publishing with print-on-demand is more cost-effective, faster, and easier than the nail-biting way publishing was done in that bygone era of the 20th century. That's ancient history now.

Back then, when you wrote your book, you sent it off to a publisher (or agent) and sat by the mailbox biting your nails, sometimes for months and months, waiting for a reply. Would they like it? Would they publish it? If the reply was negative, would they bother to say why not?

If you were fortunate enough to get an agent and have your book represented by a professional in the book business, you had a chance of getting in. But even agents get "no thank you" responses from publishers. Having acted as an agent, I remember it well.

Declaring independence

Print-on-demand is just what it says: printing that's done on demand. In other words, you write the book, you hire a printer or publisher who prints (publishes) your book – in a book format of your choosing – only when someone orders it: ON DEMAND.

YOU don't have to have thousands of books gathering dust in your dining room or garage. Instead, you turn the task of printing and fulfillment over to your publisher or printer, so you can concentrate on book #2. And on speaking engagements, or on building webinars and workshops and marketing your book across the universe.

Let me mention vanity press publishing here, because it still exists. This requires an author to buy thousands of books, at a low cost – sometimes $1-2/copy – as part of their publishing contract. The large volume lets them drive down the per copy cost of printing the books.

Let's say you hired a vanity publisher who only required 5,000 copies, a very low estimate, in my experience. For each copy, YOU do the page layout, YOU design the cover, YOU provide the proper margins, etc. Then, the printer/publisher takes a few days or weeks to produce your 5,000 copies. When you pick them up, you write a check for the balance of the cost you negotiated, and you take possession of the books. All of them.

At that point, you're responsible not only for marketing and sales, as in any publishing format, but also for storage, shipping, and handling. For invoicing and bookkeeping. Which means, you have 5,000 books sitting in boxes in your dining room, or garage. And you keep track of every book sold, where it was sold, and who bought it.

Today, there's little need to engage in vanity press publishing – unless you have unlimited free time, a car that's really good on gas, and the personality to pop into bookstores with a request to stock your book. (Don't forget that if your book doesn't sell, you'll have to drive back to the bookstore and pick it up – or, leave it there, to be relegated to the discount table … where all books go to die, eventually.)

The world of self-publishing has changed, across the film, music, and book publishing industries. The terms independent or "indie" publisher now apply fully to authors, from Stephen King to you and me!

Scott Ginsberg, author of *The Power of Approachability*, and founder of *Hello, My Name Is Scott* and *Hello, My Name is Blog*, said it best in the quote above. Now, I'm a self-published author myself. I used print-on-demand to publish my book way back in 2004, so I admit that I'm biased. I like Scott's quote (which came from an interview I did with him on my Lipsticking.com blog, January 26, 2006).

I like it, not only because he promotes self-publishing, but also because he's so right about mainstream publishing. In their world, what the author might want just is not important. Titles, page layout, book length, images, margins – they control it all. I can't even count the number of mainstream authors I know who HATE the title of their books – because they had little or no input in creating it.

Mainstream publishers normally acquire all rights to your book. Or as many rights as they can get away with – many new authors are savvy enough to negotiate audio-rights of their work, if they can't keep anything else. And even though they put thousands – sometimes tens of thousands – of dollars into the production of the book, when all is said and done, mainstream publishers expect you to market your book.

They do just enough to get their lovely advance back, and then – if it hasn't become a "blockbuster" hit – they'll walk away. Indeed, they sometimes lose confidence or interest in your book and walk away before it's published. After all, there are hundreds – no, thousands – of other authors beating on their door.

Independent publishing, using the print-on-demand model, is more than a word file uploaded to a print-shop. It's the sum-total of weeks, sometimes months or even years, of late nights at the computer composing phenomenal content; hours of research online and off; months of agony over page design and cover art; and days of battling writer's block when their test readers were pushing them to write, write, write, when they couldn't, couldn't, couldn't!

So, how do you determine which form of publishing is going to work for you? You realistically weigh your options, talk to your book coach, and make an informed decision on whether you:

- Want to retain the rights to your work
- Want to have input into the cover design and content
- Care how many copies are sold

- Are prepared to work like hell to market your work
- Are looking at possible speaking opportunities where you can sell your book in the back of the room
- Are ready to develop workshops, webinars, and other training materials based on your book

Keep in mind, no matter which form of publishing and distribution you choose, the marketing will be up to you.

Yes, we're biased towards print-on-demand and self-publishing. Our former company, Windsor Media Enterprises (we still own and use the WME Books imprint) provided print-on-demand publishing services. Yvonne was the book coach. Tom did the design and page layout. And we worked with a talented commercial printer who understood on-demand printing and who also handled our fulfillment.

We have also worked as agents for books published by big publishing companies like McGraw-Hill and Jossey-Bass. And Yvonne was a technical editor on a book about blog marketing, published by McGraw-Hill. So we do have insider experience.

But, let us just remind you of the time involvement: Mainstream print publishers can take up to 2 years to actually publish your work. If they change their minds during the writing process they can cancel the project completely. All your hard work lost. This is rare, but it happens. It happens because they own the rights. You don't.

If you're like us and thousands of other writers, your book is going to cost you in more than time and emotional energy. It's going to take some dollars and cents, too. Spend wisely.

~ Yvonne and Tom

*The **How to Write a Book** Book*

Marketing Tools and Tactics: Becoming "the Author of"

"One important key to success is self-confidence. An important key to self-confidence is preparation."

~ Arthur Ashe

Let's start with a story – once upon a time, I, too, thought mainstream publishing was the one, best way to go. I, too, slaved over my work with an eye on getting an agent and becoming a published author the "right" way.

Which meant: building credibility by having my book published via one of the big five.

These 5 colossal publishing conglomerates control 80% of books sales. They are:

1. Harper Collins
2. Hachette Book Group, formerly Warner Books of Time Warner

3. Pearson/Bertelsmann, aka Penguin Random House
4. Holtzbrinck Publishing Group
5. Simon & Schuster owned by CBS

https://stevelaube.com/who-owns-whom-in-publishing/

While I was busy daydreaming about becoming a published author, I discovered the benefits of self-publishing. Those awful days I wasted trying to get published the "right" way – I even had an agent, once – became a dim memory I wanted to forget, but couldn't.

The tears I shed, the gut-wrenching nights I lay awake wondering how I would ever get my words in print, to compete with the likes of all the authors whose books were currently sitting on my bookshelves but weren't any better than my books, floated away when I discovered print-on-demand and the value of self-publishing.

Independence Day!

It was when I decided to self-publish using print-on-demand that my book became real to me. I was transformed.

It wasn't an immediate epiphany one morning or a flat out "I'm doing this!" one evening. I only know that when I decided print-on-demand was the option for my book, *Dickless Marketing: Smart Marketing to Women Online*, words flowed like water out of my brain and onto the paper. (Well, onto the screen, hard drive, printer cache, and then onto the paper!)

I did know I couldn't wait two years for a mainstream publisher to publish it. It had to hit the market very soon after I was done writing it – it was about the Internet, and we all know how quickly things change online! Print-on-demand was my answer to that dilemma. And a good answer it was!

I wrote my book. After much research and consideration I chose my publisher, and I published my book. Of course, I hired a proofreader, an editor, and my husband did the page layout and helped with the cover design. I did my best to cover all the basics. I even paid for a press release, not because I couldn't write my own, but because at that time, the publisher was more well-known than I, so I thought the press release should come from them.

Imagine my dismay – my astonishment – my confusion, when the publisher refused to send out my press release! My book's title, so they said, "might offend some little old lady in Texas."

That's a direct quote.

The rest is history, as they say. I sent out my press release, "Look Dick, See Jane, See Jane Dominate E-Commerce" – and I got lots of attention. The book made the splash I wanted it to make, it brought in speaking engagements, and business for my new publishing company.

NO ONE cared that it was self-published.

Well okay, I have to be honest. Amazon.com didn't care. The local TV station that called to interview me didn't care. The folks who discovered my book via my website or blog, didn't (and don't) care.

The only ones who cared were the physical bookstores, because as a self-published book, it was not returnable!

Remember that: your book, that you so desperately want to get published with that big publishing house, will eventually go out of print, or just stop selling and then, and then it becomes a returnable, or "remaindered" book. As in, sent back to your publishing house, to be ground into pulp. Or, kept in the bookstore to languish in the sales bin at the front of the store. As in, deducted from any royalties you might be owed.

When you self-publish, using POD, it will never go out of print. It will never be returned to the publisher and ground into pulp. It will never be lost in the sales bin at the front or back of the bookstore. With POD, your book will continue selling as long as you continue marketing it. And, that's what this section is about: marketing your book.

Marketing Myth-busting

Let us first dispel a few myths about marketing a book.

1. *Your publisher will market your book by sending you all over the country on speaking engagements and TV interviews.* Nope. Not gonna happen. You better begin contacting TV and conference venues now, on your own.

2. *Your publisher will understand you're on the edge of fame and will want to help you step over into full limelight.* Nope. Not gonna happen. You better be famous before you start. In publishing house terms, you better have a platform and audience they can see.

3. *Your publisher has a vested interest in your book and will want to make sure it's a big success for you.* Nope. Not gonna happen.

Whatever investment your publisher put into your book was done with the expectation that you would make it a big success for them. And they will ask you to prove your marketing potential up front, in the book proposal, *before* they offer you a contract.

4. *POD is not a respected way to publish.* Not true. Indie publishing is much more respected today. But you are the one who needs to build that respect.

Just like an indie film or music producer, you're becoming an independent publisher. You need to make sure your book is professionally written, designed, and produced. It needs to be a product your readers will want to read and share. No one really looks to see who published the book.

Yvonne asked that question at a BlogHer conference once. While moderating a book panel, the question of self-publishing with POD or getting a "real" publisher came up. She asked the audience of probably 100 women who among them looked to see who the publisher was before they purchased a book. Only one hand went up.

5. *You can send your digital manuscript to your POD printer and he or she will edit, format, and create the print ready copy of your book for you.* Nope. Not gonna happen. (If it did, we doubt you'd be happy with the result.) You better get an editor and proofreader well ahead of sending your printer a digital copy of your book.

6. *Once your book is done, you can put it up on Amazon and start marketing it.* No! No! No!

You must start marketing your book the day you start writing it!

Or, two years before!

What? What kind of marketing can you do two years before you start writing your book? Let's dig into those "tools and tactics" we promised, starting with one you can most certainly start before your book.

Create a Blog

A blog is a grand tool and offers splendid opportunities to reach a wide audience. Your blog magnifies your voice through every other platform on the web.

I understand some of you may be afraid of blogging. Women I talk to think it requires a daily commitment. They worry that writing their book is enough work. Trying to write a blog, too, seems more than they can manage.

However, today, a blog is as much about video and imagery, as it is about writing. You can create videos to build a fully engaged audience and limit your writing to sharing articles or insights about your work. Including about your upcoming book!

Think of your blog as your home base online. It's where you learn to manage the growing relationships you'll be making with your customers/clients/readers. It's a way to prove and promote your expertise, and some folks even use a blog to help write their book. That daily or weekly post can be collected, after a time, and turned into a book.

Email Marketing

Email marketing is like a flower garden. You are the gardener. You decide what kinds of flowers to plant and in what order or design. Let's consider this garden to be somewhere near the house we're building.

Once planted, you tend the garden with love and care. You water it. You pull the weeds. You add new flowers and ferns or other plants and remove old ones. You watch it grow and make choices on how and when to expand it. Building personal relationship with the garden by tending to it properly helps it grow, thrive, and bring joy to you and all who view it.

It's the same for emailed newsletters or promotions. You need to understand your purpose, your goals, and your audience to get results. Not sure what to put in your newsletter? Ask. Ask your current list or a group of good friends.

A grand way to promote books is by doing a newsletter swap. It's a simple idea. You and another author agree to share each other's books with each other's newsletter lists. You will also share on social media. Appearing on someone else's newsletter list, as a guest author of that week's note, perhaps, and then offering to have them be your guest author, is a great way to promote your book and build solid relationships for marketing webinars and workshops. See below.

Today, some smart women are going back to snail mailed newsletters. There is more of an investment, given you will pay postage to send it, but the person on the receiving end will be impressed and delighted. It reminds me that everything old is new again, over time.

Be sure to include a *Call to Action* in every newsletter. What do you want your readers to do, after reading the contents? Tell them. And make it easy with a link.

Podcasting, Interviews, Conferences, Workshops, Webinars Oh My!

I cannot cover each of these marketing options in this short space. I'll touch just a bit on each one here.

Podcasting: This form of blogging is on the rise. You have two options, create your own and invite guests (who will share with you their mailing list), or connect with Kathleen Gage of *Power Up for Profits* to learn more about how to find podcasters looking for interviewees, just like you.

Yes, you may do both.

Interviews: Set up interviews about your book. Do this ahead of launch and be prepared for more after launch. Bring on experts who can speak to the topic of your book (perhaps those whom you've mentioned in the book?). Also, find ways to be interviewed, either on podcasts, blogs, YouTube or other social media channels.

Conferences: Keynote an event. Be a presenter. Find ways to sell your book in the back of the room. Bring along a few free books to gift to select people you meet.

Workshops and Webinars: Workshops are conducted offline. There is a good bit of preparation and may be some cost for these. But they are great ways to build business and sell books in the back of the room.

Webinars are training videos conducted online. You may or may not be present in the webinar. Prerecorded webinars supporting your book's purpose or message while teaching something to the audience are popular for those who cannot fit your in-person webinar into their schedule.

Conducting a live webinar can be more engaging, as it allows you to ask for and answer questions during the webinar.

Tools that are used to create webinars include Power Point, Google Slides, Camtasia, Canva. If you're comfortable on camera, go live *and* record yourself with or without slides or props to show and tell, using tools like Zoom, YouTube, or Facebook Live.

One bit of advice – always be prepared! Create a Speaker One Sheet. For an example of a Speaker One Sheet visit my Nurturing Big Ideas about page where my Speaker One Sheet is linked.

Mastermind Groups

Mastermind groups are excellent ways to gather small groups of people and serve them collectively. Build in the cost of a signed book for each member.

While I recommend a group of 10-12, many talented professionals have very large mastermind groups. These generally also offer a conference or workshop option where the group can meet in person and also meet you, their fearless leader.

Tools for hosting mastermind groups, sharing files, storing recordings and other non-public materials include private groups on Facebook or LinkedIn. There are various membership plugins for WordPress blogsites. Or for more secure private settings there are many paid platforms like Ning, Mighty Networks, or Simplero.

Tom has always liked Wild Apricot, which has a free version for your first fifty members.

For delivering live meetings or training, video services like Zoom, GoToWebinar, and Webinarjam enable private, password protected sessions.

Search online for others and test them. Find one you can use comfortably.

Marketing is Your Path to Book Sales and Success

You can see that marketing is a time-consuming task, but you cannot overlook it. You must choose which of these ideas should come before you start your book, while you are writing your book, and then, after your book is launched. Many of them will overlap.

It's up to you to make your book the best product it can be. Once you are on the path to that end, the marketing almost takes care of itself.

Getting it done!

A book coach can help you sweep all the rocks in your path out of the way. Your book coach will help you develop a marketing plan and a schedule and a way to make sure your book is done in the timeframe chosen.

Your book coach can suggest – and help you interact with – editors, cover and interior layout designers, proofreaders, and printers or online platforms, like Kindle Direct. Your book coach will keep you honest with yourself – and hold your hand from start to finish.

Marketing your book is as big a job as writing it. Do not take this task lightly. This is so-o-o **not** a "build it and they will come" undertaking. Marketing your book will determine its success. And your success, if you're using it as a tool in your business.

If you are planning to write a book this year, it's time to get serious about the entire project. Honestly, if not now, then when? If not you, then who?

~ Yvonne and Tom

Before moving on to Part 3, here's the writing outline that Yvonne gives authors. It's organized into five stages, like our 5 Step Book Building process. But in the book builder analogy, this one page outline should be viewed more as a "materials list" or construction checklist.

Another point this outline drives home: marketing runs through every stage. From selecting readers and testimonial givers, to back cover copy, to blogging about the book as you write it, to announcing its publication, to the fifth stage: *"all marketing, all the time."*

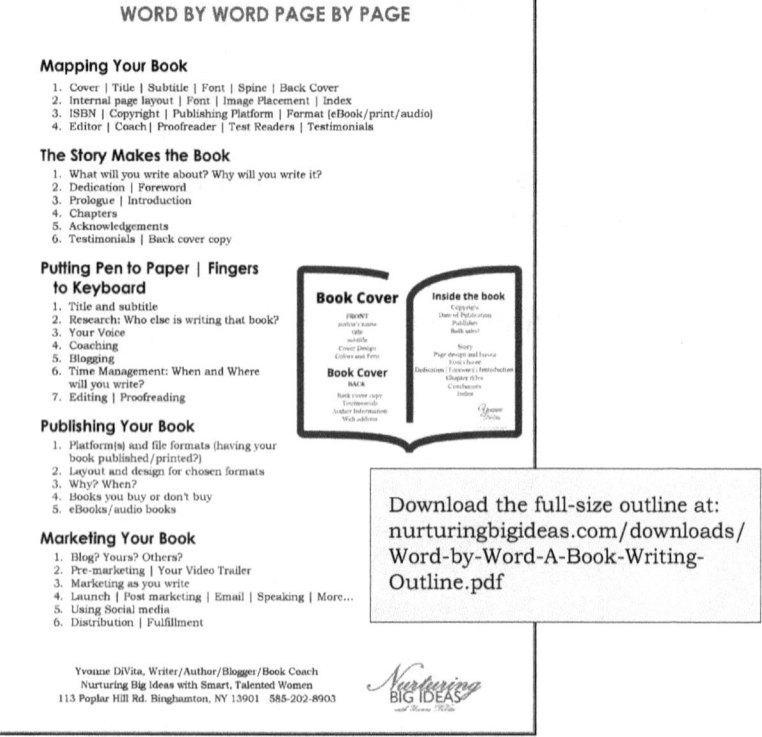

Download the full-size outline at: nurturingbigideas.com/downloads/Word-by-Word-A-Book-Writing-Outline.pdf

Part 3

Stories from the Trenches

"Once you make a decision, the universe conspires to make it happen."
~ Ralph Waldo Emerson

When I first began writing *The How to **Write a Book** Book*, over ten years ago now, I wanted more than just my own voice to be heard. In an early draft I wrote:

> I'm one little whisper in a great big universe. Each of us brings something unique and phenomenal to the writing process and to the stories we tell. That something is so important it sets each of us a little bit above the bar set by the universe – a bar that says, "Average is okay. Everyone gets by just being average."

We all know average is not okay. Not in business. Not in life. Not in our souls. The universe supports and promotes those who dare to go above and beyond.

Writers who tackle the big job of putting their souls into a book awaken the universe. They show they are serious about making their mark, about leaping over that invisible bar, becoming extraordinary – transforming themselves and their readers!

Don't do it to become rich and famous. The rich and famous myth will never die, I suppose. Writers who come to me with those stars in their eyes are told outright that I cannot make you rich and famous. Your book will only build success if you work hard at it. But even then, "rich and famous" in our pop cultural sense may still be elusive.

You will become published. You will add published author to your resume. You will show the world, the universe, your very self, that you are serious in your quest to give back to society.

That is what your book will accomplish. Your *book as business card*, or your novel, or your inspirational memoir, will build your expertise, your brand, your future – in rewarding ways nothing else can.

What follows is a group of stories I've collected over the years from other writers; from published authors who were once in your shoes. These are trusted friends of mine. These are folks who wrote books because they needed to share – share insight and expertise with the general public. Their books weren't written to make them famous or to pile up riches. Their books were created from the desire to help others become successful in life and in work by sharing their life experiences and expertise.

We all hope you'll find concrete tips to follow, lessons on what to avoid, and a whole lot of inspiration to help you "let the baby (book) be born!" – to adapt one of Tom's favorite phrases

All of the writers were kind enough to be part of this book without compensation. They understand a portion of any profits from sales of this book will go to two of our favorite non-profits: Art as Action, "an integrated performing company for artivists of all abilities" (from our Colorado days) and our local Humane Society animal shelter.

Let me start by sharing my story first.

~ Yvonne

We No Longer Live in the World of Dick and Jane

Yvonne DiVita

There I was in the early days of this new millennium. We'd survived the long-dreaded "Y2K" computer apocalypse predictions, but the 2000s had come and no one was ready for the changes ahead.

I was a web content writer, helping local small businesses by writing their about pages and their homepages. Few small business owners understood that the web was a different medium and required different forms of writing. The ones who did were not qualified to author their own content. They looked elsewhere and I was eager to help.

I also did search engine optimization. Today we all know what SEO is, but in those early days, it was mysterious and confusing. Many people avoided any thoughts of it for that reason.

I learned all I could about web content, writing for the web, using SEO, and creating content that would attract new customers for any small business.

What I discovered, in my online searching and researching, was that women were shopping online a great deal more than anyone knew or admitted to. I was shocked that more brands were not actively marketing to women, in ways that would attract them to their websites to not only discover their products and services, but to buy from them.

As I mused on that a bit, over time, I decided I should write a book about pulling people out of the old Dick and Jane world of the 20th Century, to be more successful in this new, modern 21st Century.

I was dating a marketing professional at the time and he said, "I have just the name for your book." I couldn't help but notice the gleam in his eye. He was being quite mischievous.

"Ok," I said. "What would you call it?"

He grinned. "I'd call it *Dickless Marketing*," he said.

I nearly fell out of my chair. We were in a local pizza restaurant and people were turning in their chairs to see what was so funny, but all they found was me laughing

We No Longer Live in the World of Dick and Jane
Yvonne DiVita

like a crazy woman, wondering if I had the nerve to name my book *Dickless Marketing*.

I gathered the nerve. I named it *Dickless Marketing: Smart Marketing to Women Online*, and I self-published it.

Never doubt that I knew what my title would do. I knew some folks would be offended, but I also knew, if they took the time to learn it was about giving Jane her due online, as opposed to always marketing to her brother, Dick, they would understand.

The book did cause an uproar and I was invited to interviews online and on one of my local TV stations. Funny thing is, no one wanted to say the title out loud.

My book launched my publishing company, Windsor Media Enterprises (and our WME Books imprint). It fueled my first blog, *Lipsticking* (named for a chapter title in the book), which still garners traffic and contacts more than fifteen years later.

Being an author helped me get speaking engagements around the country, and even in Canada. It became my platform and I wish I could go back and turn it into the big success it could have been, would have been, if only I'd known then what I know now.

And that is why I offer you this book and the other eBooks on my website. To save you from mediocrity. Oh, I built a strong success out of my work, and went on to even bigger things.

But I know I could have taken *Dickless Marketing* to the ends of the universe, creating even bigger success for myself, if only I'd had *The **How to Write a Book** Book*.

Yvonne DiVita
yvonne@yvonnedivita.com
Nurturing Big Ideas (www.nurturingbigideas.com)

Advice to Authors

Guy Kawasaki

Yvonne,

Here's my advice to authors for your book:

Write every day no matter what the weather, how you feel, whether the muse is upon you.

Writing is not supposed to be fun. It's pain. It's masochism.

The only thing worse than writing is not writing.

Guy Kawasaki,
Chief Evangelist at Canva
Creator of the *Remarkable People* podcast,
https://guykawasaki.com/remarkable-people/

Author of 15 books, including:
- *Wise Guy: Lessons from a Life*
- *Art of the Start 2.0: The Time-Tested,*

Battle-Hardened Guide for Anyone Starting Anything
- *Enchantment: The Art of Changing Hearts, Minds, and Actions*
- *APE: Author, Publisher, Entrepreneur– How to Publish a Book*

Sometimes a Book Just Happens

George Kittredge

How does one come to write a book, especially when they have never written one before? It has been said, although I do not know who said it, that there is a book in each of us.

For years I had suggested to many of my colleagues and friends that they should write a book. Curiously, I had never encouraged myself to do the same thing.

I was doing some volunteer business counseling work for a local business-oriented, not-for-profit organization. One of the organization leaders asked if I would be a presenter at an upcoming seminar/workshop they were planning.

The workshop was to be attended by about 30 business owners who wanted to learn how they could promote their businesses and attract clients, with only a limited marketing budget.

Having been involved in sales, marketing and business management for over 25 years, there were lots of ideas I could share with these business professionals and I enjoyed speaking in front of a group. I agreed to submit an outline as to what I would talk about.

The agreement was that if they liked it and it fit with the workshop theme, I would do the workshop. They liked my outline (eight lines on one page) and scheduled me to participate in a seminar planned for two months later.

As the date approached, I began to think more seriously about what I was going to say. It had to be entertaining, interactive, and provide each of the audience members with some lasting value. And it certainly had to be more than eight lines.

In the subsequent weeks I began to furiously write down notes, phrases, and paragraphs – anything I could think of that was pertinent to my outline. I didn't try to organize anything initially – just get my ideas down on paper.

My presentation went very well, and I was asked to do other workshops in future months. With that in mind, I continued to add more notes and thoughts to my subject

Sometimes a Book Just Happens
George Kittredge

matter. As the content began to unfold, I found it beginning to take on a life of its own.

I'm not sure exactly when it hit me, but one day while looking at all my writings it dawned on me that this had the potential of being a book.

It was at this time (about six months into the project) that I organized all my notes into chapters, came up with chapter titles and identified a main theme to weave throughout my book. The title of my book was born during a comment I made to a friend at a cocktail party.

I continued to do seminars and workshops and continued to work on my book, as my time would permit. At one point, I did not write anything for over four months.

It took me a little more than two years to finish my manuscript. The end came when I realized that I had nothing more to say. With the professional help of WME Books, a local authors-services publishing company, my book was published and released in August 2005.

My book is entitled, *THERE'S A FINE LINE BETWEEN A GROOVE AND A RUT: How to avoid a sales slump and re-energize your marketing team!*

Looking back on the entire experience, I'd like to share a few observations.

First, I discovered that with today's technology, publishing has become much more author friendly.

It makes no difference whether your book is the next best-selling novel or winds up as a gift to your family and friends. Anyone who has the desire to write can become an author using today's print-on-demand technology.

And you don't need to fill your garage with printed copies once it's published.

Second, it was most interesting to see how my book and my seminars have changed roles.

I created my book based upon my work in those early seminars and workshops. Today I am *paid* to do workshops and seminars based upon my book – and I give a copy to each person who attends.

Third, other writers often ask me what I consider to be the most important part of publishing a book.

Editing, proofreading, layout, design, artwork – all are important aspects in the publishing process.

Sometimes a Book Just Happens
George Kittredge

But what became most important to me was selecting the right publisher. It made all the difference in the world.

Finally, writing should be an enjoyable experience. And when it is – well – sometimes a book just happens.

G. D. Kittredge III

The Story Behind Managing with Aloha

Rosa Say

I love words, and I love writing them, and I have always wanted to be a writer. I grew up reading everything I could get my hands on, and very early in my life I started having this benevolent dream about another child one day reading a book I had written.

I finished the first complete draft of my book, *Managing with Aloha*, on December 21, 2003; a good four decades after my writing dreams had begun. My book is a dream come true for me, and it does chronicle a wonderful journey about a very satisfying working life of incredible lessons learned.

So, I'd really love to tell you some magical, inspiring story about it as a writer's journey. But it wouldn't be true.

I became a manager instead of the novelist I thought I'd be, opening several different hotel resorts in Hawaii. I kept writing, but

I fell in love with management, too, and it consumed quite a bit of my life.

When you read my book, I do think you'll agree that it's very passionately written; however the story behind its creation is quite a practical and unromantic one.

This is what happened:

After thirty years paying my dues, I had the big corner office of a business-woman's dreams. Huge enough to have an oversized left return executive's desk and two matching credenza-styled file cabinets, with plenty of space left over for my own conference table comfortably seating five. Big wall mirror, lush plants, soothing bubbling water fountain.

My office was on the ground floor, with two floor-to-ceiling windows framing a scenic view of tropical island landscaping. I was in the wing of a world-renowned Sports Club & Spa, and steps away from an award-winning Jack Nicklaus Signature Golf Course and luxury five-diamond bungalow-style hotel. I was vice president of resort operations for this Hawaiian paradise, and I suppose you could definitely say that I had "arrived."

And yet in July of 2003, as I stood in the center of my big beautiful corner office and looked around me, the only thought I had

The Story Behind Managing with Aloha
Rosa Say

was, "How am I ever going to get rid of all this crap in just three weeks?"

For that's how much notice I'd given my employer that I was leaving. This time, I wasn't moving everything to another office. I was done with corporate life.

In those next three weeks, anyone walking by my door would hear the steady whirring of a paper shredder. I called them in for impulsively given gifts. Second hand, but definitely very nice; a small koa bowl, framed prints, a linen box of Crane stationery, a crystal business card holder, a Levenger light wedge, Hawaiian music CDs, several Cross and Monte Blanc pens.

Still, even three solid weeks of shredding and gift-giving was not enough to dispose of, or otherwise decide what to do with, over thirty years accumulation. When it came to purely business-for-the-company stuff, I'd become an all-electronic paperless convert a long time ago, and I'd trained my staff to do the same thing so I wouldn't have to deal with what they produced. I was an exec without an admin, for I found I no longer needed one.

However, most of what I had in that office, neatly tucked away in hanging pendaflex files, three-ring binders and the most eclectic bunch of journals you've ever seen, was my writing. For as I said, I love words and I love to write. Always have, always will.

So at the end of those three weeks, I had no choice but to haul home (where I had no office at all) eight boxes of my life's lessons learned, on paper. My first thought was to scan everything, crunching it on space-saving thumb drives. But that would have taken a huge amount of time, and I quickly became more honest with myself about the fact that I'd never read it again anyway. Still, I couldn't just throw it all away – could I?

Well, I could if I somehow used it first. It was time to write the book I'd always planned to write. Once everything I needed was consolidated into one book, I could throw it away – yes, even my writing, for it would be magically transformed:

It would grow up, get edited, and get better. It would graduate. It would become my book.

So that's exactly what I did. My 266-page hardcover book, *Managing with Aloha, Bringing Hawaii's Universal Values to the Art of Business*, consolidating my thirty-year life as a manager, was written in two days short of four months time.

I settled into an energetic but comfortable and healthy routine: I was up and outside by 5:30am each morning for my 3-mile run and head-clearing, and when I walked back in the door I'd head straight for my laptop and crank out another chapter. Then I'd have breakfast, take my shower, and go back to what I'd written, and edit and re-write for another few hours.

In all honesty most of my book came from my head and not my past writing, for I had learned my management lessons, and they were second nature to me. However, if I did have to look something up in my cherished older writing I could, and I often did. And that was good enough for me.

Was it good enough for *Managing with Aloha*? I believe so; however, you can read my book and judge for yourself.

Those were probably the most productive four months of my entire life, for you get very deliberative and disciplined when you are unemployed and writing. I also say "most productive" because I've always worked hard, and I've put in some outrageously long hours, but this time I was working for myself.

At the same time, I wrote *Managing with Aloha* I created Say Leadership Coaching and went back to work, as Tom Peters' says, for "the brand called Me."

The lessons learned in my past career didn't all fit into the book, but whatever didn't fit got folded into my company business plan, and that was okay too. I developed my entire coaching strategy for a reinvention of work in between those book chapters: I wrote my new vision, my new mission, my new personal mantra, and a very detailed and comprehensive Business Plan.

I could not feel better about the creation of Say Leadership Coaching and the services it provides. *Managing with Aloha* became a better book for it too, for it's not my memoir. It uses my stories to coach you, the reader on the how-to. It became more practical and useful.

Publishing the book took a whole year more, (that's a different story) affording me the time to rewrite and edit well. But the boxes and most of what was in them did get tossed after that first completed book draft.

I do have a few more binders and some journals I still couldn't bear to part with. They take up about a yardstick's length of shelf space in my bedroom; however, their time is coming. Maybe I'll write another book.

I want to say this humbly, for I know I still have a long way to go as a writer. But I honestly feel my writing has never been better than it is now. I guess I needed those four decades of practice!

The Story Behind Managing with Aloha
Rosa Say

The writing of *Managing with Aloha* purged and celebrated the old, and it opened the door to all I still must learn, that is new.

And I keep writing. Always will.

Rosa Say is founder and head coach of Say Leadership Coaching, a mentoring, coaching and training firm created as resource for visionaries and innovators in business today. Rosa currently publishes the weekly *Ho'ohana Community* newsletter for managers and emerging leaders who are learning to foster Managing with Aloha workplaces.

Visit her at www.RosaSay.com

A Fine Position to Be In

Robert W. Bly

You can easily adapt "positioning," an advertising sales technique that will make submissions stand out on the editor's desk – and in the editor's mind.

When I worked as a technical writer at an industrial equipment manufacturer, I decided to write a book of tips and advice for fellow technical writers. Such a book hadn't been done before.

Or so I thought. Visits to bookstores and a look at *Books in Print* revealed nearly a hundred books had already been published on this rather specialized subject. How could I compete?

When I read a few of the technical writing books, I was struck by how dull, lengthy and pedantic they were. "Engineers and managers don't want a 400-page treatise on grammar and syntax," I explained to a writer friend over lunch. "What they need – and what I'd like to write – is a brief, easy-to-read style guide, a handbook they can keep on their desks and refer to when a question comes up. Something like the Strunk and White of technical writing."

As soon as I said it – the Strunk and White of technical writing – we both knew I'd found the slant that would set my book apart from the competition and sell it to a publisher. Technical writing is unfamiliar territory to most trade book editors; by comparing my ideas to the immensely popular *Elements of Style*, I made the gist of my concept immediately clear.

My coauthor and I wrote a 22-page proposal and two sample chapters. We handed this package to our agent; within three weeks he sold the book to McGraw-Hill – my first sale anywhere. The book, retitled *Technical Writing: Structure, Standards, and Style*, was published in hardcover and trade paperback and is now in its third printing. Interestingly, the publisher used the phrase "the Strunk and White of technical writing" in its press release and in a promotional flyer on the book.

I'm convinced that the book sold because we had "positioned" it. Positioning is an advertising technique that identifies and targets a product's potential buyers,

A Fine Position to Be In
Robert W. Bly

demonstrates how that product differs from the competition, and summarizes the product and its benefits by comparing it to a concept or a product that people immediately understand. In sum, positioning creates a position for the product in the buyer's mind.

Avis, for example, once positioned itself as a hard-working underdog – "We're number 2, so we try harder." Pepsi Light is positioned as a man's diet cola, while Diet Pepsi is a woman's drink.

Although we may not be aware of it, many of us use positioning in everyday conversation. Describing a new word processor to a friend, we might say, "This machine is the Rolls Royce of personal computers." The position of "Rolls Royce" connotes excellence, quality, value and high price.

Similarly, a bookstore owner described *Megatrends* to one of his customers as "the *Future Shock* of the 1980s." The customer, already familiar with Alvin Toffler's work, could now picture John Naisbitt's bestseller within the context of a familiar product.

In every book proposal, I now include a strong statement defining the book's position in the marketplace. My small-business book, *How to Promote Your Own Business* (New American Library), was pitched as "the small-business guide to advertising, publicity, and sales promotion."

Dream Jobs (John Wiley & Sons), a career guide to such "hot" industries as cable TV, computers, and genetic engineering, was positioned as "a dreamer's guide to the most in-demand careers of the 1980s and beyond."

For informational and "how-to" books, positioning can be based on the technical depth and audience interest in the subject. For example, when I wanted to write a book on computers for small businesses, I positioned my concept as management-oriented rather than hardware-oriented. I began the proposal:

> The only reason a small-business manager should buy a computer is to save his or her company time and money.
>
> The philosophy behind HOW TO BUY THE RIGHT COMPUTER FOR YOUR SMALL BUSINESS is practical and straight forward. It is this: The purchase of a small-business computer is a business decision – similar to the decision to rent office space, lease a copier, install a new phone system, or buy dictating machines for the sales force. The decision-making process for all of these situations is the same. Only the specific facts are different.
>
> So many "how to buy a small-business computer" books were on the market –

A Fine Position to Be In
Robert W. Bly

nearly two dozen at last count – that an even sharper position was needed to sell the idea. Eventually, the publisher bought the proposal on the condition that I aim the book at one specific industry. I chose a personal favorite – advertising – and my book, *The Personal Computer in Advertising*, was then published by Banbury Books.

Sometimes, positioning can make the competition work for you rather than against you. When writer Frank Evans wrote a proposal for an encyclopedia of computer technology, he positioned the concept as complementing rather than competing with existing titles in the field:

> *Computers A Through Z: An Encyclopedia of Data Processing* relates to the two major computer dictionaries, *International Computer Dictionary* (Sybex, 1981) and *The Penguin Dictionary of Computers* (Penguin Books, 1970), just as the Britannica relates to Webster's: it expands upon them. It is far more focused than such science encyclopedias as *The McGraw-Hill Encyclopedia of Science and Technology* (McGraw-Hill, 1971) in that it provides complete coverage of one specialized area of technology – electronic data processing.

To position your book, clearly identify the intended audience, show how the book differs from or complements any related books, and draw an analogy between the proposed book and something that will form a familiar, favorable image in the editor's mind.

And keep the position statement short. Someone once said that every good idea can be written on the back of a business card.

By coming up with a single, pithy sentence to summarize and slant your book idea, you break through the clutter and quickly communicate your concept to editors.

You may find yourself in a fine position to be in: that of a published author.

Bob Bly

Bob is an independent copywriter and consultant with 20 years of experience in business-to-business, financial, high-tech, industrial, and direct marketing. He's the author of more than 50 books, including: *The Complete Idiot's Guide To Direct Marketing* (Alpha Books), *Internet Direct Mail: The Complete Guide To Successful E-Mail Marketing Campaigns* (NTC Business Books), *The Advertising Manager's Handbook* (Prentice Hall).

www.bly.com

Keep On Writing

Ellen Langas

In one of the books in my *Girls Know How*® series, the fictional head of a national newspaper offers young Stephanie a final piece of advice as she embarks on a new position with her school newspaper:

"Keep on writing."

It's simple, nice advice ... for an elementary student. But that basic premise is just as well suited for the mature writer.

I discovered my own sense of logic had been my worst enemy. Often, when I would consider sitting down to write, I realized I only had 20 minutes, so I put the task off until I could find a good block of time and the right environment.

Sometimes a day would pass, sometimes a week, before I could carve out two hours to write. One day I did the math.

Typically, I complete about three draft pages in an hour. So if I spent just 20 minutes a day writing, by the end of a year, I'd have completed **three** children's book drafts.

Those little bursts of time really add up. So, much like the revered "Just do it" mantra, my revised motto is "keep on writing." I carry a notebook with me everywhere and write whenever I can.

Whether it's in the idyllic setting, typing on a laptop in a cozy chair nestled close to the fireplace, or on the back of my grocery list while I'm waiting for the tires to be changed on my car, frequent writing keeps the creative juices flowing and helps me stay in a groove.

After all, unless you actually start writing, the book isn't going to get published.

Ellen Langas is the author of the *Girls Know How*® Series

www.girlsknowhow.com

How to Write a Book Under Extreme Duress

David Young

My experience in writing a book (and really, the book isn't much bigger than a thick pamphlet) boils down to writing under duress. There's no better motivation than writing at gunpoint.

Our organization of advertising consultants (Wizard of Ads) is made up of a crazy bunch of highly creative, sometimes volatile, always interesting misfits like me. Granted, we have our saner partners and we give them the difficult task of holding onto our leashes.

One of the most difficult tasks for our founding partner, Roy H. Williams, has been to convince us that we need to become known for something, really anything. Roy knows that we have our own unique gifts and talents and has even compared our group to the X-Men. (I like that.)

One day, Roy gave us an ultimatum: Write a book in the next year or leave the partnership. The way to become known for something is to be a published author on the subject. So, pick a subject, study it, and write a book.

The hardest part for me was choosing a subject. I have a wide variety of interests but consider myself an expert in none of those areas. I stewed and sweated about the subject of my book and was rehearsing my "beg for mercy" speech for the next year's partner meeting.

Meanwhile, I enrolled in a graduate class in Cyberspace and Mass Media. There was a subject that was being mentioned quite a bit in much of the literature we were reading and when it came time to choose a topic for a research project, I decided to write a paper about blogs.

It dawned on me that this was a much more powerful form of communication than the current writings gave it credit for. I could see that a blogger had a tremendous edge in developing a reputation for good or bad. Much more than the average letter-to-the-editor-writing curmudgeon. I got a Typepad account on the day the service went from beta to full launch. In fact, my group's research report was presented in blog form.

I started blogging. Nothing very interesting, but blogging, nevertheless. I started reading blogs and it occurred to me that the most popular blogs seemed to focus like a laser on a single subject. Of course, there were blogs that rambled all over the place, but the

How to Write a Book Under Extreme Duress
David Young

folks getting notoriety were getting it for their specialist, not generalist, approach.

Ah, back to the book. I was wrestling with a half-dozen topics. Some intellectual, some humorous, some technical subjects. I couldn't decide. I even started 2 or 3 different books and abandoned each of them.

About a month before the meeting where Roy was to fire me, turn my chair to the wall, and break my plate in the fireplace, I decided to blow the dust off my research paper, flesh it out a bit and try to pass it off as a book. Sneaky, yes, but I really like these people and wanted to stay involved with them, even if I had to cheat to do it.

I had my book about ¾ finished by the time our meeting rolled around. Just to help everyone understand the subject matter, I did screen captures of about 200 different blogs, put them in a PowerPoint and set them to the song *We didn't start the fire* (Billy Joel).

I told my partners that any idiot could create a blog, and many have done so. I told them that we could use our blogs to develop our reputations. I told them that my book was almost finished, but not quite.

Their response blew me away. Roy wanted my book published right away, finished or not. Michele Miller volunteered to proof it that night. (Remember, it's not a very big book.)

I recorded *Why We Blog (and you should too!): An Exploration of the Blogosphere* the next day and was relieved that I wouldn't have to actually finish "writing" it. Michele signed up for Typepad that day and her blog, WonderBranding.com, was born.

I describe my audio book as a "Why-to" book. There is a companion workshop where we cover the "How-to" part of blogging. I don't recommend learning to blog by reading a book. If you want to blog, you can learn how on your own. The workshop just lifts you up the steepest part of the learning curve so you can get a faster start.

That's how I wrote my book. It's been a great experience and it's a super ego boost to go to Amazon and find yourself listed as the author of a book. I highly recommend it.

Bottom line: Find someone to hold a gun to your head and then write as if your life depended upon it.

Dave Young is a partner in the global consulting group, Wizard of Ads. His passion is helping business owners find the secrets to growing their company, and he's willing to stake his success to theirs. He blogs at www.BrandingBlog.com and when he's not traveling, you'll find him at work in his Wizard's Cave beneath the wind-swept prairies of Nebraska.

How I wrote *Know Your Bones*

Stephanie Siegrist

I'm definitely one of those people who'd been browsing the stacks thinking, "Look at all these books." And, "I could write a book." And, "Why hasn't anyone written a book about 'X', which led to, "I should be the one to write that book!"

I figured all of the reading and writing I've done would be enough to carry me through the process, and envisioned myself as a successful, published author.

I felt entitled to write "*Know Your Bones: Making Sense of Arthritis Medicine,*" because its content is what I talk about every day as an orthopedic surgeon.

My patients have joint pain, and they want to know how to make it go away. They also want answers to sensible questions about what pill to take and why, what side effects they should watch for, how to get the best results, and, most importantly, what's right for them.

The few minutes my patients and I have during appointments is not enough time to launch into an accurate lesson they would retain. So, I'll write them a book!

Easier said than done! The process has been a fantastic education in the publishing industry and creating an appealing (and profitable!) consumer product.

Once the first draft was written, the most important work was about to begin. Didn't I write this book so others would read (and buy!) it? How will I put it in their hands? Didn't I want to make a difference in the readers' health? How would this book help them, and be different than all of the other information swirling around?

If you know enough about a certain topic to fill a book, you can't know enough about formatting, editing, design, production, copyrighting, cost accounting, distribution, and promotion. Give your book the expertise it deserves and find good help.

Fortunately, there are books about books. Along with classes, websites, and other sources, you'll get the big picture about writing and developing your project.

However, you can't do everything else well, by yourself, in order to make this book a reality. You'd have to learn another profession and spend time making and

How I wrote *Know Your Bones*
Stephanie Siegrist

following up on contacts. You'll need someone else's expertise, like a book coach.

Expect to pay for this expertise.

But you'll gain tremendous value in a better-quality book, with wider distribution, and sell more copies than you could on your own.

Stephanie Siegrist, MD

https://www.urmc.rochester.edu/orthopaedics/general/doctors.cfm

It's Enough to Give You Gas

Michele Miller

Since the publication of *The Natural Advantages of Women*, a surprising number of comments I've received have not been about the topic of the audiobook. The book deals with differences in the female brain.

But many people ask instead about the accomplishment of even writing a book in the first place.

"It must come easily to you," some have said. "Writing must be in your blood."

"How do you do it? You're so lucky – it must be great to just sit down and have the words flow onto paper."

Nothing could be further from the truth.

When asked by my publisher to write an audiobook, I froze like a deer staring straight into the headlight of an oncoming train. For some time, I had been percolating ideas about women and their special "powers," such as intuition and nurturing. But the task at hand was so overwhelming I nearly walked away from the project altogether. Most people do, when presented with a challenge that doesn't have an immediate resolution.

If you've been thinking of writing anything – a book, article, or even an important letter – you may be shying away from the "unknown," as in what to expect the first time you sit down to write. You may be blocked on how to even begin.

Let me share my personal experience about trying to get my own audiobook off the ground. I had some general ideas, but not a solid foundation upon which to build them. In what would later prove to be a repetitious cycle, I had to go through what I now call "The Gestation, Labor, and Delivery of a Brain Burp."

In clinical terms, there are six basic steps:

Step 1: Shock

Physical Manifestations: Frozen body parts, wide eyes, open mouth.

Common Phrases:

"You want me to do what?!"

"You want it when?!"

"Are you sure you don't have me confused with someone who can actually do this?"

Step 2: Delusion

Physical Manifestations: A combination of ego and excitement creates a lack of oxygen to the brain, leaving one feeling a little heady.

Cocky mannerisms creep in, such as winking at everyone like you know something they don't.

Common Phrases:

"I have a very special take on the world. Millions have been waiting to read what I have to say, and they don't even know it yet. Let me at 'em."

"Lunch? Oh no, I couldn't possibly, darling. You see, I'm busy writing a book."

Step 3: Denial

Physical Manifestations: Sitting slumped over, head in hands. Brain constipation.

Sometimes accompanied by extended bouts of procrastination.

Common Phrases:

"What ever possessed me to think that I could put two sentences together, let alone write a book?"

"Have I ever had an original thought in my life? I am a lemming ... just point me in the direction of the nearest cliff."

"I wonder if there's anything good on the Weather Channel ..."

"It's official – I'm an idiot. I couldn't write my way out of a paper bag."

Step 4: Anger

Physical Manifestations: Pacing, muttering to oneself. Often involves the throwing of dishware.

Common Phrases:

"Just who got me into this mess, anyway?"

"I must have been out of my mind to agree to do this."

"Agree to do this? I was forced ... !!"

"Somehow, this is my parents' fault ..."

Step 5: Surrender

Physical Manifestations: Slouched back in chair, arms hanging down. Staring straight up at the ceiling with mouth open.

It's Enough to Give You Gas
Michele Miller

Common Phrases:

"I give it up, I give it over."

"Uncle, uncle, uncle."

"I'm dyin' here."

Step 6: Breakthrough

Physical Manifestations: Lying prostrate on floor. Low, intermittent moaning.

Common Phrases:

"I am no more significant than the dust mite that just crawled inside my nostril."

"What is wrong with me? Is it my wiring?"

"Wiring... wiring... brain..."

"Brain... brain... my brain... female brain....."

"Hmmm... I wonder....."

And a brain burp is born.

You'll know a brain burp when you experience it, because suddenly you can see, hear and smell a little more clearly. It's as though all the tiny puzzle pieces that have been floating around in the back of your mind magically "click" into place.

You might even be like me, ending up with a completely different picture than originally planned.

If you think you have the intestinal fortitude to subject yourself to this cycle because you have something important you want to tell the world, then you're meant to be a writer. And you will be a writer, given enough time and thought.

Just be ready to ride that roller coaster of angst during each phase of the writing process. Like any great thrill ride, writing is scary, but holds the promise of big rewards at the other end. Like popcorn. And cotton candy. And burping to your heart's content.

Michele Miller

On Writing

Andrea Learned

My writing career snuck up on me.

Interestingly, now that I am more focused on writing, what I write about seems to sneak up on me too.

Anyway, here's the story:

I went through high school and college and graduated without much passion for any particular thing (but had a happy life, nonetheless). One thing that had been easy for me throughout my education was writing, and I must have just taken my talent for granted.

Thankfully, my mom was an English writing instructor at the community college level during those years. So whenever she'd check over something I was writing for a class, she'd say, "Andrea, you *really* are a good writer."

Over time, I think it was the compounding effect of her words, in addition to the fact that

I kept heading into work that included writing – like public relations and marketing – that steered me toward writing as a career.

The final shove came when I wrote an article in hopes that it would help promote the work of the marketing firm I had co-founded. I tentatively submitted it to my favorite online business newsletter and waited all of five minutes to get a reply back from the editor.

She was immediately very interested in having me write regularly for the publication, and that was that. The contract for my first book, *Don't Think Pink* (which I co-authored), came two years or so after that.

Having an existing portfolio of published work for both that online publication and an e-newsletter I had created were key in landing that opportunity.

My advice to writers who may need a nudge: Figure out how to get yourself writing regularly. Even if it takes creating your own publishing medium – like a blog or an e-newsletter.

Being able to point potential agents and publishers to an existing and easy-to-access body of work is very helpful in building legitimacy. Plus, you will find that your topics, for books or articles, tend to evolve from your daily writings.

On Writing
Andrea Learned

You'll be surprised to see that some of your book-developing research happens without your even focusing on it.

Rest assured, even given all my writing experience, I still have days where I need to email an article or chapter to my mom just to hear her say, "you ***really are*** a good writer."

In fact, I'm pressing send now.

Andrea Learned

www.learnedon.com

The **How to Write a Book** Book

Lessons about Writing That I Keep Forgetting

Dick Richards

The challenge of writing a book is as much about the process as it is about the content: maybe more. I'm a process kind of person, so I pay a lot of attention to it.

Over the last ten years, four books, and dozens of articles I've noticed seven lessons about which I must keep reminding myself. I can't seem to learn them for good and when I forget them I get in trouble.

Here they are:

1. Every Sentence Is a Doorway

When I put a period at the end of a sentence, I usually treat it as a signal to move on. That is all wrong. A period at the end of a sentence ought to be a signal to ask questions about the sentence.

Take this sentence as an example: It is dangerous to seek to possess knowledge.

I need to remind myself to ask questions like these:

- What is knowledge? How does one try to possess knowledge?
- In what ways is it dangerous? Why did I say "dangerous" instead of "silly" or "fruitless"? Is seeking to possess knowledge silly and fruitless as well as dangerous?
- What examples do I have of the danger of seeking to possess knowledge? Why did I say "seeking to possess" instead of just "possess"? What are all the meanings of the word "possess"?

There are a lot of questions in even the shortest of sentences. If I remember to ask myself questions like that about every sentence, and then answer those that seem relevant and interesting, I have a book.

2. Put Your Butt in a Chair and Stay There Until the Words Come

I am great at distracting myself. There is always someone to call, someplace to go, some website to explore, a dog to walk. So, it is important for me to schedule appointments with my book; times when I pay attention to it even if I do not feel inspired.

Lessons about Writing that I Keep Forgetting
Dick Richards

Sit down. Stay there.

Don't answer the phone. Don't wander into the kitchen to make tea.

Once, a friend came knocking at the front door of my house and I didn't answer. Two-hour blocks of time work for me. My true friends understand and forgive me.

3. Make the Work Portable

Along with staying in my chair, I also find it useful to think of everywhere I go as an extension of my writing space. I have discovered ideas in malls, on turnpikes, on riverbanks, in the woods, at dinners, and in many other places.

When working on a book, I try to remember to carry a small notebook everywhere and a recording device in the car.

4. Mindless Activity Can Be Useful To the Mind

When conscious awareness is engaged in writing, the subconscious is also at work. We can't hear what goes on in the subconscious because we are filled up with mental activity.

Breaks from the mental activity allow the subconscious to burst into conscious awareness. These breaks ought to be relatively mindless. A long walk works well for me. So does a long drive.

I forget this when my need to think of myself as a busy guy gets in the way.

5. You Can Write While You Sleep

Another way that I put my subconscious to work is to pay attention to my book just before I go to bed.

I might read what I wrote that day. I might start a new section or chapter; just a few sentences or notes.

When I remember to do that, getting started the next day is much easier. Often, I can't wait to get started.

6. Don't Talk Away the Energy

When I am writing a book, lots of people want to talk with me about it. Some are just curious, some sincerely want to be helpful, and some want me to write the book that they wish they were writing.

Lessons about Writing that I Keep Forgetting
Dick Richards

Many writers gain energy from such discussions. I often don't.

I need to be careful about whom I talk with, about what aspect of my writing I discuss, and about what point in my process the discussion takes place. If I talk with the wrong person at the wrong time, or about the wrong aspect of my writing, I lose some kind of vital energy that I need in order to write.

7. Manage the Process

Writing isn't one single process. It isn't just banging out words. There are lots of varied activities involved: research, editing, reading what I have already written, brainstorming, making outlines, formatting text, and so forth. There is a lot to do.

Usually, when what I am doing isn't moving the work forward, and I am feeling frustrated or even just bored, it helps to shift from one activity to another.

If I can remember how writing works I can better manage the work of writing.

Now that I have collected these lessons that I need to remember, maybe I won't forget them as easily. Don't bet on it!

But maybe you will learn them for good and avoid needing constant reminders.

Good luck with that.

Dick Richards has authored several books, including: the award-winning *Artful Work, The Art of Winning Commitment,* and *Is Your Genius at Work?* Today, you can find him at www.DickRichards.com where he showcases his artistry in abstract painting.

7 Steps to Accidental Writer Success

Amy Shojai

As writers, we wear several hats. In my case, all the hats are furry ones and usually come with music.

I graduated college with a theater and music/performance major and really never intended to become a writer. I planned to go into performance, but instead fell in love and married – and had to find a "real job." Sounds familiar, doesn't it? How many of our "plans" get stymied by detours? In my case, it turned out to be a fortuitous one, because the job working at a veterinary clinic in the mountains of Eastern Kentucky changed my life and ultimately gave me a writing career.

I used to tell my mom all about the various fun, scary, heartbreaking and amazing experiences that happened with the cats and dogs at work. She told me I should write them down. I'd tried to write a mystery (it was truly awful!), but nonfiction hadn't been on my radar. So, I compiled my stories into an anthology and submitted to publishers.

I hadn't a clue what I was doing. This was before Email or the Internet with all correspondence by snail mail. I collected so many rejections that I could have wallpapered my house with them. Sound familiar? I nearly gave up – but then the librarian pointed me to a three-year-old copy of Writers Market. I found pet magazines and submitted chapters of my book as articles.

I collected even more rejections because I hadn't read any of these magazines. I hadn't done my homework. Finally, the editor of Dog Fancy took pity, and wrote me back the BEST REJECTION LETTER EVER! It told me 1) I was a talented writer, (cue the happy tears), and 2) why the story was rejected.

This generous editor gifted me with the answers to questions I'd neglected to research.

#1 Tip: Be a mentor!

They're the heavens' gift to starry-eyed hopefuls and can make dreams come true.

The next submission about my own dog was closer, she said, but needed XYZ, and she gave me the opportunity to fix it. When I submitted the rewrites – it sold. Oh, y'all reading this know that thrill of a first sale.

Did I mention how much I admire and love mentors? I sold eight articles in a row to that editor, and thereafter to other pet magazines.

And then lightning struck when a New York book publisher called me out of the blue to write a cat book. They'd read my magazine articles and tracked me down from the bio-note. Over the years I got two more book deals in the same way when editors read my articles and tracked me down to invite me to write for them.

I even wrote one book after I lost a writing contest when the judge tapped me for a future book. And I sold 100 previously published print articles to one of the first online ventures when they asked, for a nice chunk of change years later.

#2 Tip: Include bio-notes and contact information in everything you write

You never know where that can lead.

I still wanted to publish fiction, though, and submitted to dozens of agents with little success. Between submissions, music and theater performance assuaged the writing drought.

One agent finally replied "no thanks" to the fiction (drat!) but liked my nonfiction.

Together we sold a dozen pet books to New York publishers.

#3 Tip: Be flexible

Dreams come to those who see the reality within the sparkly vision.

Then the nonfiction book well dried up, and I believed my career was over. My agent couldn't give away my nonfiction books, and many went out of print. I sulked. I pouted. I pounded a head-shaped dent in my office wall. I took a "real job" and taught high school choir for a semester. When I finally got tired of the pity party, I reinvented myself.

Theater and music fed my starved soul, so I co-wrote, produced and performed in *KURVES, THE MUSICAL*. The agent got rights back from my out of print books, so I updated and re-issued in new formats, including Ebook versions and audio. And they sold! Holy cats.

#4 Tip: Look for opportunities in the disappointments

If my books hadn't gone out of print, I'd never have gotten back the rights, which enabled my re-birth as an author.

#5 Tip: Creativity breeds creativity

What other creative avenues feed your muse? Writers paint word pictures, composers sing symphonies of sound, and actors bring it all to life.

Nourish your creativity.

Suddenly, no nonfiction deadlines stood in the way of fiction, other than my "day job" teaching choir. The book I'd always wanted to read, I now had the time to write – before class, during lunch, and after school.

So, I wrote a thriller featuring an animal behaviorist with a service dog viewpoint character (and a cat, of course) that my existing nonfiction audience would embrace.

I made plans to self-publish LOST AND FOUND.

#6 Tip: Leverage your expertise

What you do in your "real life" when incorporated in your writing work can potentially bring you closer to your personal brass ring goal.

Because of the internet, writers and authors no longer struggle alone and can reach out for help and support in many ways. That's how I connected with the folks who helped publish my backlist nonfiction titles, and (oh thank you doG!) also agreed to publish my thrillers.

And that opened even more doors for me as a reinvented fiction author.

#7 Tip: Ask for help

Just as it makes YOU feel awesome to be a mentor, graciously accept such gifts from others. Connect with and build support groups with others who share your goals and experiences.

It took me more than 20 years of hard work to "accidentally" hold my first fiction book, *LOST AND FOUND* in my hot lil' paws. But that led me to publish several more.

And now that I've got a firm grip on that shiny ring, I'm not letting go. This past year, I took another scary step and left that small publisher to update and release all my nonfiction and fiction books under my own FURRY MUSE PUBLISHING imprint.

Today, there are many paths to publishing, and no "right" or "wrong" way to get there. I hope these 7 tips help you reach out and capture the dream that's close to your heart.

Find more about Amy Shojai at www.SHOJAI.com

I dropped in a dragon, a car crash, a winning lottery ticket...

Robbi Hess

"I'm going to write a book!" How many times have you said that? How often have you heard others say that?

How many people do you know who have the follow-through?

I write for a living. I'll bet, on most days I average 6,000 words per day, that's probably a conservative estimate because I didn't factor in social media work I do, or emails I answer or editorial calendars I write.

The year I announced "I'm going to write a novel," it was an audacious goal. It scared the hell out of me. Naturally, I made the announcement on social media – I mean, where else does one let the world know they are going to write a novel?

Apparently, I am not the writer who is going to sit in her isolated turret pounding away on the vintage typewriter keys, bleeding words onto the page.

NaNoWriMo

It was seven-years-ago I discovered National Novel Writing Month (NaNoWriMo). During November participants proclaim they will write an entire 50,000-word novel. These 50,000 words equates to 1,667 words per day, every day, in November.

That should be a breeze for me, right? After all, I average 6,000 words a day.

Fiction words are more difficult than nonfiction words – to me, anyway.

The first year I joined NaNoWriMo, I "failed." I only wrote a 30,000-word novel. I petered out at a little over mid-month. My story was going nowhere.

I tried to shove my character into new actions. I dropped in a dragon, a car crash, a winning lottery ticket… These didn't work.

I was writing a paranormal romance that had no lottery tickets, no dragons and the only car crash was the novel and its romance!

The characters despised one another. Frankly at 30,000 words I despised them as well. I declared I was quitting, closed that document, shoved it in a folder and forgot about it. I licked my wounds, went back to writing my nonfiction and lived happily ever after... until the next October rolled around.

For several years, I continued participating. I completed the novel. But eventually I shoved the novel in a virtual drawer and moved on with my life.

The Story Bible

In October 2018, I developed a plot for my new November novel. I built a world. I created characters who didn't annoy me. I populated their lives with rescue pets and this time I added magic.

I had a cover designed because I wanted that physical inspiration. I developed a story bible. When November 1 arrived, I was ready.

Fingers poised over keyboard and away I went. I toiled on my 1,667 words every day. I hit the milestones NaNoWriMo participants shoot for. I attended write-ins and mingled with other wanna-be novelists.

By the 45,000 word mark I was running out of steam. My story had been wrapped up in a bow... great, right? Wrong. The goal is 50,000 words.

I refused to "fail" again. I stopped writing where I was because I was truly at "the end" of the story.

My characters needed more trouble thrown at them. I needed to find a way for the heroine's magic to come at a cost.

I decided to give her migraine headaches each time she used her magic. There were some sections of the book in which she'd too readily call up her magic to solve a problem. She took the easy way out.

Now, with the "I'm going to get a migraine if I do this" twist she had to think long and hard on whether using magic was worth the price.

Bewitched!

Imagine you're Samantha from *Bewitched*. You're probably not old enough to remember that 1960s show, but in the show Samantha could twitch her nose and viola her problem (whether it was having to cook a four course meal for ten guests with no more than fifteen minute notice or having to get her husband Darrin out of a jam) disappeared or resolved itself. I don't remember Samantha ever suffering any ill effects from using her magic other than her husband forbade her to use it.

I dropped in a dragon ...
Robbi Hess

Yet, he allowed her to use it when it got him out of said jam.

Since *Bewitched*, I have learned magic has a price. It's something that is "known" in the paranormal world. If magic had no price, then anyone who was magical could use it willy-nilly and have no consequences. Hence, my main character had to find a non-magical way out of her problems, until only magic could get her out of it.

On those occasions she used magic the reader knew my character had already exhausted other options and they were rooting for her to use magic for heaven's sake! This connection with her was because they'd seen her use magic for something silly like whipping up a batch of cupcakes because she had a sweet tooth only to be laid flat by a migraine.

When she was suffering the migraine, her pets suffered because she wasn't paying them any attention – this, too was something she never wanted them to feel again – abandoned.

I sprinkled in issues. I added conflict. I upped the ante on using magic. The readers were on edge wondering what would push her to the tipping point of magic, then BAM: another migraine.

This novel topped out at 51,045 words! I'd won! What did I do with that completed novel? Life, a new puppy and a new grandbaby took time away from my fiction, but it's back on track and has been front of mind for some time now.

I Learned...

Once I pulled that word doc back up, after I regained control of my schedule, I determined my 50,000-word November 2018 novel would be the first book in a three-book series of cozy mysteries.

I had a genre I loved, characters I adored, rescue pets, magic ... And. A. Plan!

I finished my novel in 2018. I've been working on it, editing it, polishing it and making it publishable as the first in my three-part series.

I learned readers want more than one book. It behooves the cozy mystery author to have all three books ready to go and ready to be released within a month or two of one another.

Am I going to wait another entire year after I complete the November 2019 novel?

No. I am committed to this three-book series and to seeing it published and in the hands of readers by mid-2020.

I dropped in a dragon ...
Robbi Hess

Bottom line: My suggestion for How to Write A Book?

1. Know your why. I honestly will not feel complete in my writing career if I don't publish more fiction.

2. Have a plan. If I can write 1,667 words of fiction a day, every day in November, there is no reason I cannot do this year-round, am I right?

3. Announce it to the world. Accountability matters, people.

4. Even if you're a "pantser" if you're a newbie novelist, you may want to have some sort of a plan – even a loose one.

5. Remember that even if you "fail" like I did the first year, it's okay. I remind myself that I wrote 30,000 words on a novel. I DID what other people only say they will do. That makes me NOT a failure.

Nonfiction and writing nonfiction books is something I can do, have done and continue to do.

Fiction writing and publishing novels has been a want, desire, dream and something I cannot wait to complete. I know, just like when I used to regularly write and publish confession stories, that once I get on a roll, there will be no stopping me!

What's stopping you?

Robbi Hess
30 Minute Solopreneur
www.facebook.com/robbi.hess

Best Laid Plans (Or, Writing Lessons from HGTV Stars)

Tom Collins

Yvonne and I are big HGTV ~~addicts~~ fans. She loves the design and decor aspects. I do, too. But for me, the functional parts fascinate more. Like, can they remove that wall? How can they fit in another bathroom? Will that landscaping provide proper drainage?

We live that stuff, as well. We've been together 16+ years and owned six homes. We've always enjoyed "recreational house hunting" days together, even when we're not in a buying mood.

And as dozens of realtors could attest, I rarely walk into a house without thinking out loud, "Well, that wall's gotta go . . . we could add two bedrooms and a bath in the unfinished basement . . . would this work as your office, if we cut a door here?"

So now you know where our Book Building analogies come from! My own experiences in writing my book last year confirm the value in those analogies.

So I thought I'd bookend our *How to Write a Book* lessons with a few specific examples from the HGTV stars we enjoy most.

Write the book you're living in

I'd been meaning, intending, planning, starting, outlining, researching . . . you get the idea . . . two other books, when it finally dawned on me that *Read 'Em & Reap* **insisted** on being written first.

That's the only way I can describe the experience. From within my research on learning, positive psychology, healthy aging, longevity, multi-generational workplaces, and more – intended for the other books – *Read 'Em & Reap* simply jumped the line and started pouring out of my head.

In HGTV terms, the lessons come from shows like Scott McGillivray's *Income Property* and the emotional ties to their existing home that most people show on *Love It or List It*. For those unfamiliar, Scott's show revolves around helping homeowners who need extra income find space within their existing home, or larger ones they're looking to buy, and then transform the "found" space into a rentable unit.

On *Love It or List It*, "Designer Hilary" and "Realtor David" work with couples who disagree about whether their existing home

Best Laid Plans (Or, Writing Lessons from HGTV Stars)
Tom Collins

should be remodeled to work better for them, or sold so they can buy a new one. I'd estimate over 60% of the couples "love it" due to their emotional attachment to the home, the neighborhood, the memories.

A lesson from both shows applies to your book building project: there's value to be found . . . and revealed . . . and shared, in the "place" you're living.

You have knowledge and experience that can help others, whether through a nonfiction book like mine, or in the characters and plot of your novel. Think of it as finishing that basement rental unit, adding that in-law apartment for a family member, or upgrading that kitchen for your own enjoyment.

The property you need for your project – intellectual property – is right there in the life you're living. You will probably need to acquire some new material to complete it. But look for the foundation and blueprint of your book in your past or current life experiences and let it come out.

Start with a plan, or steal one

For this lesson, we turn to Jonathan and Drew Scott, the *Property Brothers*. I love the way Jonathan creates 3-D renderings of how the various rooms in the rehabbed house will look when the project is completed.

As to the stealing, Drew often takes clients into an upscale neighborhood to show them real world examples of homes with their "must have" features. And then reveals how much over their budget it would cost to buy them move-in-ready! From there, Jonathan tells them how he can deliver those same features in a fixer-upper house.

These techniques work in book building. I started by "stealing" my outline from a blog post on The Muse, *5 Science-Backed Reasons Why Readers Do Better in Their Careers*. The post provided some "must have" features, but little more, devoting less than 500 words to all five combined.

Then, like Jonathan, I incorporated them into my first draft TOC, but didn't stop there. I added a sixth benefit of reading uncovered in my research and opened up a wider focus, far beyond the career benefits of reading.

With that plan in hand, I was ready to build and wrote my way to a completed manuscript, all laid out in Adobe InDesign and ready for . . .

In-progress "reveals" and unplanned revisions

That's when I sent the galley out to a handful of "readers" to get their feedback

Best Laid Plans (Or, Writing Lessons from HGTV Stars)
Tom Collins

and, hopefully, recommendation blurbs for the cover! Among them, Pamela Wilson, who had agreed to write a foreword.

Pamela read the galley overnight and wrote back saying she loved the book, but . . . she, somewhat cautiously, expressed her wish that I had spent more time on the tips for getting more reading into our lives. And on what to do with all that knowledge gained.

Her feedback birthed three new chapters, with entirely rewritten and expanded content.

My own daughter asked me a question about what I meant by "deep reading." Which forced me to do more research, discovering I hadn't known all that term implied. That added knowledge became the Preface.

Look at this stage as being similar to when experienced flippers, say Tarek and Christina on *Flip or Flop*, have a realtors-only open house to get feedback on their work. Or when Jonathan's sometimes hovering clients tell him – well into the project – that they want a bigger island in the kitchen, or maybe find out they need a nursery!

Or when Chip Gains opens a wall on *Fixer Upper*, discovers hidden *shiplap*. If you watch the show, you know what's coming. His wife and partner Joanna gets to call in the owner and get approval to reuse the shiplap on the feature wall in the family room!

In my case, the feedback I sought out revealed some serious problems in the "foundation" and "floorplan" of my book. So I went back to the keyboard and added three new rooms to the floorplan (Chs. 7-9) and deeper footings under the foundation (the Preface).

All in all, I added around 25% to the length of the main text. In construction terms, that's like adding another 500 sq. ft. to a standard ranch for an in-law apartment, or a luxury master suite.

Get feedback as soon as you have enough to "reveal" and be open to change the floorplan, create new shop drawings, and rebuild your book. Your "as-built" version may not – probably should not – adhere too closely to the original blueprints and floorplans.

Who's your project manager?

We described the role of a project manager in construction as "a pro who can make sure the work is progressing smoothly and being done right." We noted that for book building, filling that role may require you to hire a book coach.

It could be you. *If* you have the skills and experience to run the project yourself, to know when to hire, how to choose, and are

Best Laid Plans (Or, Writing Lessons from HGTV Stars)
Tom Collins

ready to manage the cast of book specialists we talked about in Parts 1 and 2.

In my case, I work with Yvonne. She's an author and has acted as a developmental editor for authors, technical editor on a book with a large traditional publishing house, and agent on multiple traditional publishing books and proposals.

She's also wrangled all the book design, publishing, and marketing roles (often, that meant me!) on a couple dozen books during our publisher days. Together, we value the HGTV approach!

Consider the HGTV stars again. "Designer Hilary" has done hundreds of home makeovers. Yet she employs a project manager.

Although they do some of the physical work themselves, Tarek and Christina employ a general contractor/project manager. Theirs usually visits the house they are considering with them, before they even decide whether to invest, and then runs the renovation when they are not on site.

You might have all, or most of the design, editorial, publishing, and marketing skills you'll need – in addition to being a writer. Or like me, you might live with or be able to partner with someone who complements your skills and fills in the ones you lack. I like to think of us as resembling Chip and Joanna!

But recognize the danger. Don't be like a "star" on the show *Disaster DIY!*

The lessons from that series apply to book building, too. If DIY is your only option, then by all means, do your book that way.

Learn and apply all the book building tools and techniques you can master. Find the help you need where you can. Get your book done and out there.

But don't let yours be anything less than it can be, out of any sort of false DIY pride.

Tom Collins
Author, *Read 'Em & Reap: 6 Science-Backed Ways Reading Puts You on the Road to Achieving More and Living Longer*
www.OldDogLearning.com

Index

A

Anderson, Chris 36-37
  TED Talks: the Official TED Guide to Public Speaking 36
Armstrong, Erika
  A Chick in the Cockpit: my life up in the air
  cover design 48
Ashe, Arthur
  quote, key to self-confidence 81
Audio book 132, 137-138

B

BlogHer conference panel
  self-publishing survey 86
Bly, Robert W.
  A Fine Position to Be In 121-126
  Dream Jobs 124
  How to Promote Your Own Business 123
  Internet Direct Mail: The Complete Guide To Successful E-Mail Marketing Campaigns 126
  Technical Writing: Structure, Standards, and Style 122
  The Advertising Manager's Handbook 126
  The Complete Idiot's Guide To Direct Marketing 126
  The Personal Computer in Advertising 125

Book
  book idea 3
    as foundation 15
  format
    eBook 1
    hard cover 1
    power of a print book 14
    print book 1
    soft cover 1
  marketing 8, 21
  publishing 8
    print-on-demand 8
    self-publishing 8
    traditional publishers 9
  writing
    satisfaction 4
    who can/should 1
Book Building 13
  blueprint 16
    chapter titles 16
    mindmap 16
    outline 16
    story board 16
    table of contents 16
  downloadable outline:
    5 Step Book Building process 94
  exterior design
    back cover 19
    consumer behavior driven 20
    cover design 19
    curb appeal 19
    front cover 19
    spine 19
  floorplan 17
    change orders 17

feedback and revision 18
flow 17
shop drawings 17
idea as foundation 15
interior design 22
  as-built drawings 22
  furnishings 22
  graphic elements 54
  indices, endnotes, references 24
  justified margins 53
  notes 22
  overall visual impact 53
  page headers 22
  signage, visual cues 22
  table of contents 22
project manager 28
  book coach 29
Book Coach 29
  collaborative partner 70
  guide 70
    choosing publishing options 79
  liaison with other service providers 70
  pitching in to fill role(s) 70
  range of writing and publishing experience 70
  role description 70
    analogous to building project manager 70
Books in Print 121
Breaking Out of Writer's Block
  create something new 42
  find relevant news stories 42
  focus elsewhere 42
  get inspiration from reading 41
  get some exercise 42
  let your subconscious work 42
  rework your TOC 42
  start planning your index or reference list 42
  take a break 42
  talk with someone 42
Breaking Out of Writer's Block 39

C

Carroll, Lewis 13
  Alice in Wonderland 13
Collins, Tom
  Best Laid Plans (Or, Writing Lessons from HGTV Stars) 167–174
  Beyond Words: The Role of Graphics in Legal Writing 54
  No Justification
    2005 blog post 63
  OldDogLearning.com 174
  Read 'Em & Reap: 6 Science-Backed Ways Reading Puts You on the Road to Achieving More and Living Longer 168
Conferences 90

D

DiVita, Yvonne
  Dickless Marketing: Smart Marketing to Women Online 83
  downloadable outline:

Index

5 Step Book Building process 94
Lipsticking.com blog 76
Nurturing Big Ideas website 90
We No Longer Live in the World of Dick and Jane 101–104
Your Book as Business Card ebook 68

E

Editing 67
  breaking rules for effect 67
  copy editing
    rewrite/revise 68
    role description 68
    style consistency 68
    transtitions 68
    wordiness/jargon 68
  developmental editing
    accepting judgment 69
    example 69
    role description 68
    stand in/up for readers 69
  fool for a client 67
Emerson, Ralph Waldo
  quote, the universe conspires 97
Estes, Deanna
  book cover designer, interview 51

F

Facebook Live 90

G

Gage, Kathleen
  Power Up for Profits 89
Getting Started 33
  begin with TOC 36
  daily writing commitment 33
  digital format 34
    ease of editing 34
    necessary for publishing 34
    required by editor/coach 34
  throughline: "electifying" your idea 36-37
  writing, not engraving 37
Ginsberg, Scott
  blog interview 76
  Hello, My Name is Blog 76
  Hello, My Name is Scott 76
  quote, what sells, not what's good 73
  That Nametag Guy 73
  The Power of Approachability 76
Gladwell, Malcolm 40
Grammarly.com 68
Graphic Elements 54
  adjacent in space, with text 55
  color 57
    RGB vs. CMYK 58
  dimensions 57
    legible and readable 57
  dots per inch, dpi 56
  grayscale 56
  image editing software 59
  image format 58
    filename extensions 59
  image quality 55
  image sizing and resampling 59

resolution 56
vector vs. raster images 59

H

Hess, Robbi
  30 Minute Solopreneur 166
  facebook.com/robbi.hess 166
  I dropped in a dragon, a car
      crash, a winning lottery
      ticket 159–166
HGTV 167
Holleley, Douglas
  *Digital Book Design and
      Publishing* 63
Hyatt, Michael 40

I

Interviews 89

J

Justified Text 60
  ragged beauty 63
  unjustifiable 60

K

Kawasaki, Guy
  Advice to Authors 105
  *APE: Author, Publisher,
      Entrepreneur - How to
      Publish a Book* 106
  *Art of the Start 2.0: The Time-
      Tested, Battle-Hardened
      Guide for Anyone
      Starting Anything* 106
  chief evangelist at Canva 105

*Enchantment: The Art of
    Changing Hearts, Minds,
    and Actions* 106
Remarkable People
    podcast 106
Wise Guy: Lessons from a Life
    105
Kingsolver, Barbara
  quote, chain that muse 43
King, Stephen 40, 76
  On Writing 40
  cover design 47
Kittredge, George
  Sometimes a Book Just
      Happens 107–111
  THERE'S A FINE LINE
      BETWEEN A GROOVE
      AND A RUT: How to
      avoid a sales slump
      and re-energize your
      marketing team! 109
Klein, Naomi
  No Logo
    cover design 47

L

Langas, Ellen
  Girls Know How® series
      127–128
Learned, Andrea
  Don't Think Pink 144
  On Writing 143–145
Lee, Marshall
  *Bookmaking: Editing / Design /
      Production* 55, 61
Lickerman, M.D., Alex
  quote, amateurish cover
      design 46

Index

quote, wrappers affect how we react 45
Lofts, Norah 40

M

Marketing 85–94
  blog as a marketing tool 87–88
  book marketing myth-busting 85–87
  email marketing 88–89
  how a book coach can help 92–93
  mastermind groups 91
  selective time commitment 92
  speaking opportunities
    podcasting, live or online events 89–90
    speaker one sheet 90
Miller, Michele 131
  It's Enough to Give You Gas 137–142
  The Natural Advantages of Women 137
  WonderBranding.com 132
Munier, Paula
  A Borrowing of Bones
    cover design 49

N

Naisbitt, John
  Megatrends 123

O

Oates, Joyce Carol 40
On Being Phenomenal 26

P

Podcasting 89
Power of a Visual World 45
  judging a book by its cover 45
Printers 58
  print proofs, necessity for 58
  RGB vs. CMYK color 58
  working with 58
Proofreading 67
  breaking rules for effect 67
  fool for a client 67
  near the end 70
Publishers
  agent role 74, 78
  independent or "indie" publisher
    comparison to film, music industries 75–76
    Yvonne's journey 81–84
  mainstream publishers
    control title, design, layout 76
    expect author to market 76
    limited marketing budgets 76–77
    purchase all rights to book 76
    take up to 2 years to publish 78
    the big five 81–82
  print-on-demand 73–74
  traditional or indie publishing 71
    fixing mistakes after first printing 71
    higher standard for indie authors 71
  vanity press publishing 74–75

weighing your options 77–78
checklist 77–78

R

Reedsy.com 68
Richards, Dick
  Artful Work 152
  DickRichards.com 152
  Is Your Genius at Work? 152
  Lessons about Writing That I Keep Forgetting 147–152
  The Art of Winning Commitment 152
Robbins, Prof. Ruth Ann
  quote, isn't much justification 53

S

Samulack, Donald
  blog post discussing justified text 64
Sandberg, Sheryl
  Lean In
    cover design 50
Say, Rosa
  Ho'ohana Community newsletter 119
  Managing with Aloha, Bringing Hawaii's Universal Values to the Art of Business 116
  Say Leadership Coaching 119
  The Story Behind *Managing with Aloha* 113–119
Schopenhauer, Arthur 28

Schriver, Karen A.
  Dynamics in Document Design 64
  quote, manually space lines 62
Sevilla, Christine
  Information Design Desk Reference 64
Shojai, Amy
  7 Steps to Accidental Writer Success 153–158
  FURRY MUSE PUBLISHING imprint 158
  SHOJAI.com 158
Siegrist, Stephanie
  How I wrote *Know Your Bones* 133–136
Smith, Elinor
  quote, happen to things 33
Stories from the Trenches 97–99
  Amy Shojai
    7 Steps to Accidental Writer Success 153–158
    ask for help 158
    be a mentor 154–155
    be flexible 156
    best rejection letter ever 154
    find opportunities in disappointments 156
    include bio-notes and contact information in everything you write 155–156
    leverage your expertise 157
    nourish your creativity 157
  Andrea Learned
    advice: get writing regularly 144

Index

create your own blog or newsletter 144
Don't Think Pink 144
existing portfolio of published work 144
On Writing 143–145
you really are a good writer 143
average is not okay 97
David Young
  audio book 132
  How to Write a Book Under Extreme Duress 129–132
  Why We Blog (and you should too!): An Exploration of the Blogosphere 132
  writing at gunpoint 129–131
Dick Richards
  don't talk away the energy 150–151
  every sentence is a doorway 147
  give attention to your book just before sleep 150
  keep your butt in the chair 148
  Lessons about Writing That I Keep Forgetting 147–152
  let your subconscious work 149
  make the work portable 149
  questions to ask about every sentence 148
  write while you sleep 150
  writing process includes: research, editing, reading what I have already written, brainstorming, making outlines, formatting text 151
Ellen Langas
  how to "keep on writing" 127–128
George Kittredge
  ease of print-on-demand technology 110
  from book to paid speaking 110
  from workshop outline to book 107–109
  selecting the right publishing partners 110–111
  Sometimes a Book Just Happens 107–111
Guy Kawasaki 105
  Advice to Authors 105-106
  the only thing worse 105
  write every day 105
Michele Miller
  anger 140
  breakthrough 141
  delusion 139
  denial 139
  It's Enough to Give You Gas 137–142
  shock 138
  six steps to delivering a book 138–142
  surrender 140–141
  The Natural Advantages of Women 137

writing as a "brain burp" 138–142
writing is scary, rewarding 142
more than one voice 97
Robbi Hess
　characters needed more trouble 162
　five bottom line writing lessons 165
　I dropped in a dragon, a car crash, a winning lottery ticket 159–166
　NaNoWriMo, first year fail 160
　NaNoWriMo (National Novel Writing Month) 160–164
　unlike *Bewitched*, magic has a price 163
Robert W. Bly
　A Fine Position to Be In 121–126
　Dream Jobs 124
　How to Promote Your Own Business 123
　make competition work for you 125
　positioning in a single, pithy sentence 126
　positioning your book in editors' minds 121–126
　Strunk and White of technical writing 122
　Technical Writing: Structure, Standards, and Style 122
　The Personal Computer in Advertising 125

Rosa Say
　book and business plan 117–118
　decades of practice 118
　manager instead of novelist 113
　Managing with Aloha, Bringing Hawaii's Universal Values to the Art of Business 116
　The Story Behind *Managing with Aloha* 113–119
　using stories to coach the reader 118
　wirting routine, energetic, comfortable, healthy 116–117
Stephanie Siegrist
　creating an appealing product 134
　education in the publishing industry 134
　expertise your book deserves 134
　find good help 134
　How I wrote *Know Your Bones* 133–136
　knowledge as an orthopedic surgeon 133
Tom Collins
　Best Laid Plans (Or, Writing Lessons from HGTV Stars) 167–174
　Chip and Joanna Gains, *Fixer Upper* 172
　don't star on *Disaster DIY* 174

Index

Hilary Farr and David
 Visentin, *Love It or List It*
 168–169
if DIY is your only option
 174
in-progress "reveals" and
 unplanned revisions
 171–173
Jonathan and Drew Scott,
 Property Brothers
 169–170
reader feedback birthed
 three new chapters and a
 preface 171
revise your floorplan, create
 new shop drawings, and
 rebuild your book 172
Scott McGillivray, *Income
 Property* 168
start with a plan, or steal one
 169–170
Tarek El Moussa and
 Christina Anstead, *Flip
 or Flop* 171
Tarek El Moussa, *Flipping
 101* 174–175
who's your project manager?
 173–175
write the book you're living
 in 168–169
variety of publishing paths
 97–99
Yvonne DiVita
 blog marketing 103
 help from experience
  103–104
 launching a publishing
  company 103
 titling *Dickless Marketing*
  102–103
 We No Longer Live in the
  World of Dick and Jane
  101–104

T

The Muse blog
 *5 Science-Backed Reasons Why
  Readers Do Better in
  Their Careers* 170
Throughline: "Electrifying"
 Your Idea 36-37
Toffler, Alvin
 Future Shock 123
To Justify, or Not 53
Tufte, Edward 55
 *The Visual Display of
  Quantitative Information,
  2nd ed.* 63
 Visual Explanations 63
Twain, Mark
 quote, actions speak 39
Typepad 130, 132

W

Williams, Roy H.
 Wizard of Ads 129
Wilson, Pamela 171
Workshops and Webinars 90
Writing
 blogger 3
 book coach 3
 daily 33
 digitally 33
 inspiration 7

writer, as identity 2
writing process 7, 15-28, 151

Y

Young, David
　How to Write a Book Under
　　Extreme Duress 129
　*Why We Blog (and you should
　　too!): An Exploration of
　　the Blogosphere* 132
YouTube 90

Z

Zoom 90

About the Authors

The "Tom and Yvonne" husband and wife show began almost 20 years ago when two business consultants met at a networking event and soon discovered an equal passion for books, writing, reading, and helping other people flourish.

They formed a print-on-demand publishing company, Windsor Media Enterprises, aka WME Books. Yvonne became the developmental editor, book coach, and salesperson, while Tom was the designer for the books, inside and out, along with managing the production end.

At the same time Yvonne and Tom were growing their publishing business, blogging became a 'thing'.

All WME authors were encouraged to blog and a new line of business emerged, WME Blogs and the Business Blogging Bootcamp. The AHA group at WME (authors helping authors) became experienced in building blogs and teaching others how to use them as a business tool. Yvonne's *Lipsticking* blog remains active, more than fifteen years later.

In 2009, a new big idea popped up while talking with a few other professionals. Influencer marketing – with pet bloggers. BlogPaws was born and grew in influence over 10 years. During that time, WME was closed and all focus was given to BlogPaws. A couple of years later, the influencer company was acquired by a much larger company, which, in turn, was acquired by PetSmart.

Just before BlogPaws, the two entrepreneurs had moved from NY to CO. While in CO, they moved homes three times. Their final move was to a house that was framed but not finished, giving them the chance to add their touches, and make it their own. Afterwards, completely by himself, Tom finished the 1500 square foot basement to include more living space.

Though the two loved CO, family back home called. In 2018 they packed up and moved back to upstate NY.

Today, their home is another work-in-progress. Life experiences led them to combine their writing efforts to offer this book, The **How to Write a Book** Book, as a testament to their continued love of books and writing, and their vagabond nature of moving and remodeling homes.

On the experience side, both writers are published authors online and offline.

Yvonne is a developmental editor and book coach. Find her via www.NurturingBigIdeas.com.

Tom is a Chief Guide Dog at Old Dog Learning. His latest book, **Read 'Em & Reap** is his testament to the power of books and reading to improve, even extend, lives.

You can find them online daily. If you write and they don't reply, they are likely out walking their dog, Emily.

Looking for more?

Yvonne's website has a range of free and for sale ebooks and other resources aimed at helping women and authors bring their BIG IDEAS (whether it's a book, a new business, or beyond) to life. You can browse at:

https://ulearn.nurturingbigideas.com/

Tom's book can be found on Amazon.com or directly on his Old Dog Learning site:

www.olddoglearning.com/old-dog-learning/books.html#tombook

www.ingramcontent.com/pod-product-compliance
Lightning Source LLC
Chambersburg PA
CBHW050526170426
43201CB00013B/2102